NEW LEFT THOUGHT
An Introduction

THE DORSEY SERIES IN POLITICAL SCIENCE

NEW LEFT THOUGHT

AN INTRODUCTION

LYMAN TOWER SARGENT
University of Missouri — St. Louis

1972   THE DORSEY PRESS, Homewood, Illinois   60430
Irwin-Dorsey Limited, Georgetown, Ontario

First Printing, April 1972

Library of Congress Catalog Card No. 71–187061
Printed in the United States of America

To LINDA

PREFACE

In the following pages the reader will find a brief introduction to the ideas of the movement known as the New Left. No such introduction has been available before, and the need for one has been obvious. Whether one considers it from a purely North American perspective or as a worldwide phenomenon, the New Left is with us, having a daily impact on the lives of many of us.

The reader should be aware of what this book is and what it is not. I have attempted to present the central ideas of the movement. I have focused on the youth movement and the movement writings rather than on the intellectuals who have developed these ideas. I believe it is valuable to try to capture the movement now with all of its naïveté, its brilliant insights, and its sometimes crystal-clear and sometimes muddled thinking, while it is still developing. Therefore I ignore many writers who would be included in a different sort of analysis. But I have attempted to present the movement as its exists, not as we might like to see it.

This gives a much different picture than another analysis would produce—a more confused picture and a more radical one. Undoubtedly I can be accused of ignoring streams in the New Left, even in the youth movement, that are more conservative than the main outlines I present. Although they are treated briefly in Chapter 7, the general avoidance is intentional. I emphasize the radicals because they predominate in the thought of the movement and because I find them more interesting and instructive than the "moderates" or the "reformers." Also, I deal briefly with two parallel movements, black radicalism and the women's liberation movement, because of their contemporary importance.

In addition, although I deal with traditional concepts in social and political thought, the approach necessarily blends theory and events, philosophy and institutions, doctrine and movements, because this gives the most accurate picture. Since it is likely that in the future more extensive analyses and evaluations will be made, this book can be seen as a first step toward understanding a movement that is much discussed and only little understood.

I shall present the basic ideas using the same format in each chapter. First, I shall briefly discuss the generally accepted use of the concept. Second, I shall present the movement's critique of contemporary society as it relates to the concept. Third, I shall present the New Left version of the concept.

I have tried to be objective because I think that we must try to understand as completely as possible before we evaluate. However, I am in sympathy with the goals of the movement, which are after all the goals of Western civilization. At the same time, I oppose its growing tendency toward violence, although I believe I can understand it.

This book has been extremely difficult to write. The movement is elusive; its goals tend to be very general and lacking in specifics, hence hard to pin down. The New Left is made up of innumerable parts, both groups and individuals, which seem on one level to be in fundamental disagreement on many issues; and the difficulty of achieving accurate generalization has been formidable. Finally, the movement is changing, and I have at times felt as if I were chasing a single leaf blowing in the wind with many other leaves. If there are errors in what follows, I am solely to blame for them. That which has merit is due in large part to the help of many friends and colleagues. I wish particularly to thank my friends and colleagues in the Department of Political Science at the University of Missouri—St. Louis, who endured the birth

pains of this book and discussed many aspects of it with me—
particularly Frederic Pearson, Stuart Lilie, Joyce Lilie, Kenneth
Johnson, and Werner Grunbaum. I also wish to thank Profes-
sors J. G. A. Pocock, James F. Doyle, Peter Fuss, and Elizabeth
Clayton, who commented on an early paper on the New Left
I presented to the St. Louis Area Conference for the Study of
Political Thought. Finally, I wish to thank Professor Norton
Long who persuaded me to take on this task and prodded me
with his always challenging questions.

March 1972   LYMAN TOWER SARGENT

CONTENTS

1
INTRODUCTION

Traditional moral standards are changing throughout our society; students are demonstrating against duly constituted authority; marijuana is fast becoming as widely used a drug as tobacco and alcohol; the American success ethic is being challenged and many people—most of them young, but many middle-aged—are dropping out of conventional ways of life to form communes in cities and in the countryside. These are facets of what is happening in the United States today, and often such changes are attributed to the activities of the New Left. But not everything that is changing *is* related to the New Left. The drug culture and the New Left are not identical, certainly; many commune members are ambivalent about New Left activism; not all demonstrating students are of the New Left; and far from all those who are challenging traditional moral standards belong to the New Left.

Problems of definition and approach

The "New Left" is a label that has been attached to and largely accepted by a wide variety of groups and individuals who desire radical change in contemporary society. (The word "radical" comes from the Latin word *radex,* meaning roots; the New Left desires basic changes in the very roots or foundations of society: therefore it is radical.) The New Left is "new" because it has, for

1

the most part, rejected the dogmas of Marx and his followers—the "Old Left." In fact, much of the thinking of the New Left is reminiscent of pre-Marxian socialists such as Robert Owen and Etienne Cabet.

It is impossible to define the New Left precisely, since many of the individuals and groups that seem to agree on the basic ideas and traits outlined in this book are not happy about labels. Others, who sometimes identify with a particular label, do not seem to fit the labeled category in any way except by their use of the label. Therefore, in the pages that follow I have tried to lay out the common elements of New Left groups, and this is as far as it seems safe to go by way of definition.

The New Left is not united. There may seem to be some unity in the demand for radical change, but a glance at the specifics of priorities and tactics immediately dispels the sense of unity. It is rarely possible to find any cohesion in the New Left by looking at the *specifics* of either goals or tactics.

It is possible to find cohesion at another level, however—the level of generalized goal and symbol. The New Left does, on the whole, have a set of commonly held, generalized goals and symbols. The New Left without exception but with varying emphases believes in participatory democracy, equality, liberty, and community. Each of these general goals will be considered in turn in this book to see what specific content can be found for each. There is just enough cohesiveness to provide an approach to the study of the New Left, and an organization for this book, but the reader must constantly keep in mind that there is also great diversity and many disagreements. It would be a mistake to see either just the cohesiveness or just the diversity and disagreements —both are there and both are strong.

In order to fully understand any movement, it is necessary to delineate, as specifically as possible, the society it wants to create. In addition we want to know how it wants to get from here to there, and this point, the tactics necessary to bring about change, is currently the most divisive point exercising the New Left. In fact, it often seems as if the New Left has become mired in the same kind of ultimately sterile debates over tactics that helped emasculate the Old Left.[1]

Finally, we want to know why so many want radical change. The New Left is clearly growing in spite of all its ideological splits and divisions. Partly this is because many of its symbols and goals are part and parcel of Western heritage and are, therefore, quite appealing. The New Left's enemies, and they are many and vehement, fail to understand it, and often attack it in ways that only serve to strengthen it. Change always comes too slowly and the faults of the democratic process are all too obvious. Thus, no matter how well-intentioned, the day-to-day activities of politicians and policemen, presidents and professors invariably strengthen the numbers of the New Left.

The appeals of the New Left are numerous and must be carefully understood in order to grasp the significance of the movement. The primary appeals are in the New Left's goals, most of which come from the stated values of Western civilization—liberty, equality, justice, peace—but which are everywhere dishonored or ignored. Every child in North America is raised to accept these values—at home, in school, in church or synagogue, and by the mass media. He is told that we (and, it is often implied, *only* we) believe in and have achieved these goals. Given these circumstances, to grow up and see how far we actually are from achieving these goals is a shock. The divergence between myth and reality and the shock of discovering this divergence create many radicals and cynics. At the same time, however, it should be pointed out that many people at other times or living under other political systems have recognized the disparity between myth and reality and have become neither radicals nor cynics.[2]

---

[1] See the selected bibliography at the end of this book for some suggested readings on the Old Left.

[2] Although it is not the purpose of this book to examine the reasons for the adherence of so many to the New Left, some of them will be noted from time to time. For further material on this subject, see among others, Kenneth Keniston, *Young Radicals: Notes on Committed Youth* (New York: Harcourt, Brace & Jovanovich, 1968); Seymour Martin Lipset and Philip G. Altbach (eds.), *Students in Revolt* (Boston: Houghton Mifflin,

Living with a movement, it is difficult to stand aside and look at its growth and development and the ideas and events that inspired it. But perspective is essential to full understanding, particularly so because it is something that modern radicals tend to lack. This is not the place for a detailed history of the New Left, though it is essential to try to grasp the Movement's background, nor is this the place to put the New Left into the perspective of the Old Left.[3] It would be easy, for instance, to demonstrate that there is nothing really new under the sun—that it was all, or almost all, said first by Owen and Cabet, or the Cyrenaics and Cynics of Ancient Greece—but doing this would not negate the worth or contribution of the Movement.

Let it be understood, however, that none of the positions discussed here are as simple as they are presented. Generalizations help define the background of the New Left, but it must be kept in mind that they are generalizations and that they represent complex ideas and relationships.

The existentialist background

During and immediately after World War II the main current of interest with respect to the New Left is the growth of existentialism. While many in the New Left have only the foggiest notion of what existentialism is all about, some thinkers who were existentialists or who were closely allied to that philosophic school, particularly Albert Camus, are precursors of the New Left and helped provide the climate that enabled the New Left to grow.[4]

Although it became known as a philosophy of despair, exis-

1969), originally published as the Winter 1968 issue of *Daedalus;* and Richard E. Peterson, "The Student Left in American Higher Education," *Daedalus,* XCVII (Winter 1967), pp. 293–317.

[3] Brief notes in this direction are made in the Conclusion.

[4] Writing in 1966 Jack Newfield noted that even with ". . . an appalling anti-intellectualism among the newer SDS [Students for a Democratic Society] members," most of them had read Camus. This, however, no longer seems to be the case. See Newfield, *A Prophetic Minority* (New York: New American Library, 1966), p. 87.

tentialism was never simply that. World War II, the revelations of German atrocities at the end of it, the bomb, and the Cold War that followed it led men to despair, to believe that perhaps life wasn't worth living. This feeling was important, but more important still was the growing conviction that even if suicide were rejected, life could have no meaning.

The basic points of importance relevant to existentialism and an understanding of the New Left can be summarized as follows:

1. Existentialists argued that there could not be certainty about anything. In particular it was impossible to know of any purpose or meaning in or to life. As Camus says, ". . . all true knowledge is impossible."[5]
2. This belief tended to lead to despair.
3. Despair, though, was not the only possible answer. Meaning can be *created*.
4. We create our own meaning or purpose through our *actions*.
5. We are individually responsible for the values we create by our actions. (This burden of responsibility could lead to despair, but did not have to.[6])
6. Men's actions should reject murder in all forms, should assert the value of all men, and should move toward the establishment of world peace and prosperity.[7]

Probably the most important influence of existentialism on the New Left is the stress it placed on action rather than thought. This helps account for the anti-intellectualism found in the New Left, though it is worth noting that anti-intellectualism was not dominant among the existentialists. Combined with the notion

---

[5] Albert Camus, *Le Mythe de Sisyphe; Essai sur l'absurde* (Paris: Gallimard, 1942), p. 26.

[6] See Jean-Paul Sartre, *L'Existentialisme est un humanisme* (Paris: Nagel, 1966), trans. by Bernard Frechtman as *Existentialism* (New York: Philosophical Library, 1947).

[7] The literature on existentialism and its social and political implications is enormous. For a short selection of titles, see the bibliography at the end of this book.

of rebellion as the mechanism for establishing values,[8] the stress on action helps establish the most basic assumptions of the New Left.

The movement background

Of course, all responses to the post-World War II era did not take the positive direction of acting to create meaning or purpose. Some individuals sought refuge in a search for new thrills and pleasure. Others found solace in the Oriental religions, particularly Zen Buddhism. The search for pleasure, Zen, and existentialism blended in the Beatniks.

The Beatniks

"Many proper middle-class people, and most of the magazines, dismissed the Beats as unwashed, bearded exhibitionists. In fact, they were the vanguard of social and cultural revolution. . . ."[9] The Beatniks were the first dropouts. They were the immediate forebears of the hippies and the communal movement. They were the direct descendants of the bomb and despair. "Then comes the day of the Laodicians when you know you are wretched and miserable and poor and blind and naked, and with the visage of a gruesome grieving ghost you go shuddering through the nightmare life."[10] They sought physical pleasure as their first response to despair. ". . . to him sex was the one and only holy and important thing in life."[11]

This picture is accurate and it is the one adopted by the mass media, but it is at the same time a distortion because it is not the whole picture. Even in Kerouac's *On The Road* there are suggestions of something more, as can be seen in the meaning of

---

[8] To understand this idea, consult Camus, *L'Homme revolte* (Paris: Gallimard, 1951), trans. by Anthony Bower as *The Rebel; An Essay on Man in Revolt* (New York: Vintage Books, 1956).

[9] Michael Harrington, "Introduction," Jack Newfield, *A Prophetic Minority* (New York: New American Library, 1966), pp. 9–10.

[10] Jack Kerouac, *On the Road* (New York: New American Library, 1957), p. 89.

[11] Ibid., p. 6.

the word "beat." "He was BEAT—the root, the soul of Beatific."[12] Most observers missed the point that "Beat" came from "beatific," with its implications of rapture and its hint of religion. The beliefs of the Beats can best be seen in Allen Ginsberg's *Howl* and Kerouac's *The Dharma Bums.*

Howl was meant, in part, to shock and outrage middle-class America. Ginsberg wanted to shake Americans out of their lethargy and apathy and force them to recognize that there was much wrong with this country. The Beatniks' life style, like Ginsberg's poetry, was a challenge to middle-class Americans. In their rejection of country, God, money, and cleanliness, the Beats attacked the symbols of faith of the American middle class. The direct parallels to the hippies are obvious, though, on the whole, the Beatniks were less concerned than the later hippies to present a positive side to their life style. They sought pleasure and a sense of community with those who felt as they did. They shared material goods among themselves but seldom talked economics. Their primary concern was to live a life of pleasure and in doing so to protest against the apathy and grim seriousness of their contemporary America.

In *The Dharma Bums,* Jack Kerouac reflected another important side of the Beats. The Dharma bums were interested in Oriental religion, particularly Zen Buddhism, which stressed a nonrational, anti-intellectual approach to life. Zen taught that man's rational faculties were insufficient to bring him enlightment or true understanding, and it accepted physical pleasure. Many Beatniks adopted the Zen approach and when they did turned toward a somewhat different style of life than they had been living, one which included contemplation and meditation. As Alan Watts points out in his book *Beat Zen, Square Zen and Zen,*[13] they did not grasp all the meanings of Zen, but many followed their own version of it, such as that expressed in *The Dharma Bums.*

---

[12] Ibid., p. 161.

[13] Alan Watts, *Beat Zen, Square Zen and Zen* (San Francisco: City Lights Books, 1959).

. . . see the whole thing is a world full of rucksack wanderers, Dharma Bums refusing to subscribe to the general demand that they consume production . . . I see a vision of a great rucksack revolution thousands or even millions of young Americans wandering around with ruck-sacks, going up to mountains to pray, making children laugh and old men glad, making young girls happy and old girls happier, all of 'em Zen Lunatics who go about writing poems that happen to appear in their heads for no reason and also by being kind and also by strange unexpected acts keep giving visions of eternal freedom to everybody and all living creatures. . . .[14]

Through many routes—Zen, settling down in urban com-munities with other Beats, or returning to the "straight world"— the Beat generation slowly dwindled and vanished. But its ideas were to be picked up and developed by the hippies.

The Civil Rights Movement

Many of the people who would otherwise have been attracted to the dwindling ranks of the Beats found an alternative in politi-cal activism. The energies of American youth shifted rapidly from despair and pleasure-seeking to justice-seeking. Having discov-ered that all was not right in the American Eden, they found something to do. They flocked into the South to help their black brothers win integration, and in doing so they found hatred, vio-lence, and death. Many became disillusioned with American de-mocracy. They had believed that the American political system would rapidly respond to a cause that was so obviously just, and it didn't.

The Civil Rights Movement was a holy crusade for many American youth. They had finally found something they could do that was obviously good, true, and beautiful. They poured their vast energies into righting the wrongs of centuries within a few years. Put that way it is obvious that they could not hope to suc-ceed, but they had been taught that the United States' political

---

[14] Kerouac, *The Dharma Bums* (New York: New American Library, 1958), pp. 77–78. Copyright © 1958 by Jack Kerouac, The Viking Press, Inc.

system was the best in the world and would respond to a just cause, and they acted on what they had been taught.

For a time it seemed as if changes might take place. John F. Kennedy was elected President and the Peace Corps and VISTA were founded, new avenues for youthful energies and desires. But Peace Corps and VISTA volunteers were told not to rock the boat too much or upset local political leaders too much, and they gradually became disillusioned again.

Then John F. Kennedy was assassinated and for a time Lyndon Johnson carried on his crusade and some things *were* done: poverty was discovered in Eden and a war was proclaimed against it. But gradually enthusiasm waned, this crusade faltered too, and the money went into a different type of war.

The Anti-War Movement

The Anti-War Movement started with the Free Speech Movement at the University of California in Berkeley. The Free Speech Movement was originally part of the Civil Rights Movement. It was directed toward removing the restrictions against students' freedom to propagandize for their political views on campus, but it rapidly led to the same sort of confrontation that had been faced in the South. This was the students' first realization that the problems that concerned them were not simply regional ones but were indeed national ones. And students became more and more frustrated, more and more violent.

As the war in Vietnam escalated, so did opposition to it. Draft files were destroyed, men opposed and evaded the draft, and lie-ins and sit-ins temporarily blocked troop and weapons movements. Politically, the war or its conduct was opposed by many in both major political parties, but with little effect. With the start of the 1968 Presidential campaign Eugene McCarthy became a rallying point for the dissident, antiwar groups, but McCarthy ran a poor campaign (despite the dedicated efforts of his many supporters), Robert Kennedy was shot, and the Democratic Convention came to Chicago.

For many American youths, the violent events in Chicago

changed them from peaceful protest against the war to active rebellion against the system. This is not the place to detail those events, but they signaled the beginning of large-scale militancy. Broken heads and lungs seared by tear gas became the badges of a new revolutionary generation. From this point on the rhetoric became more militant. Very few had talked of revolution before Chicago—many talked of it afterward.

But after the 1968 elections a surprising breathing spell occurred. Things quieted down to a truly remarkable extent. And then came Kent State. The four students killed at Kent State joined a growing list of Movement martyrs, but they were the first white students shot down in the North, and of course America's blacks noted that the reaction to their deaths was much greater than to the many previous black deaths, or even to those a few weeks later at Jackson State, a black school.

Kent State seems, however, to have been a major breakwater of the Movement. Some reacted by going underground to become professional revolutionaries, keeping up pressure through bombs and sabotage, becoming urban guerrillas. Others, seeing a need for different tactics, settled down for a long revolution, with their life styles their major weapons. Some dropped out to rural or urban communes. Many hopes of a quick, violent revolution died at Kent State, but a deep-seated, enduring hatred of the system was born.

The United States will live with the consequences of the events at Chicago and at Kent State for many years.[15]

---

[15] Two chronologies of the Movement exist. One, focusing on student unrest from 1964–68, can be found in Julian Nagel (ed.), *Student Power* (London: Merlin Press, 1969), pp. 225–35. The other, a more general one covering the period 1954–68, can be found in Massimo Teodori (ed.), *The New Left: A Documentary History* (Indianapolis, Ind.: The Bobbs-Merrill Co., 1969), pp. 477–82.

2

THE SEARCH FOR
THE AUTHENTIC SELF

It is possible to begin a description and analysis of the New Left at a number of different points, such as community (the prime goal), action (the prime means), equality (the first cause the movement took up), or participatory democracy (supposedly the Movement's major contribution to political thought). Or one can turn to a problem that has particular importance to youth movements—the question of the authentic self or authenticity.[1]

Alienation

One of the most common criticisms of contemporary society, from Marx to the hippies, is the charge that the life style demanded by society alienates, or cuts off, man from himself, his fellows, and his work. Marx founded his criticism on the working of the economic system,[2] but more recent thinkers have rejected his analysis as too narrow. The causes of alienation are undoubtedly

---

[1] For a treatment of the question in an earlier period with considerable comment on its contemporary relevance, see Marshall Berman, *The Politics of Authenticity; Radical Individualism and the Emergence of Modern Society* (New York: Atheneum, 1970.)

[2] Marx's comments are found in his *Economic and Philosophic Manuscripts of 1844* which have become the most influential Marxian text today. It is available in many editions.

11

diverse, from the awareness of the lack of any objective meaning in life suggested by Camus to the notion of powerlessness suggested by Charles A. Reich in *The Greening of America* (1970).

Whatever the causes, alienation is generally considered to be a major or even the dominant condition of contemporary life. The word "alienation" means cut off from, separated from. Thus the word implies some sort of disconnection between things or the feeling of aloneness or separateness that has been described so often in contemporary literature.[3] In addition, there are the three distinct subcategories of alienation that were mentioned above— the alienation from self, the alienation from others, and the alienation from work.

Man alienated from himself

The alienation from self can be seen in part in modern man's concern with and seeming inability to answer the question "Who am I?" To ask this question without being able to answer it means that man cannot find in himself any base or foundation upon which to build his life. On one level he is the "other directed" discussed in David Riesman's *The Lonely Crowd* (1951), or one who takes his values primarily from his peer group and has no values that he has thought out and created for himself. On another level he is Camus' Meursault in *The Stranger* (1942), who is not even aware of his own existence or the existence of the world around him. The alienated man is cut off from an awareness of self.

Perhaps one of the most basic characteristics of the alienated man is that he is unaware. The existentialist writers usually argue that the first step beyond alienation is the development of awareness. First man must become aware of his own situation; then he must react against it and overcome it.

---

[3] See Gerald Sykes (ed.), *Alienation; The Cultural Climate of Modern Man,* 2 Vols. (New York: George Braziller, 1964).

The man who is alienated from himself can find no meaning in his life, no standard for existence. Life does not seem to be worth living because he cannot say *why* he is living. If he asks the question, he tends to answer that he simply does not know. He has no answer. He has no meaning in life.

The man who is alienated from himself cannot find a role in life that he finds acceptable. Since he has created nothing for himself but has simply been put into or accepted roles that are not of his own choosing, he is usually vaguely dissatisfied with life. He has been formed by a system external to himself. He finds that the role or the roles that he has are one-sided, that they create a "one-dimensional man," to use Marcuse's phrase. There is no coherence to his roles. He is not a whole person, and there is no joy in his life.

Man alienated from his fellows

The alienation of an individual from others is a somewhat easier notion to grasp. We recognize it all around us every day in the breakdown of family ties, seen in but not limited to the well-known generation gap, and in the breakdown of the ties that form communities. There are very few of the traditional neighborhood groupings that were common 50 years ago. Many people rarely see and never speak to their neighbors. Apartment houses are series of isolated units. There is no feeling of community even among immediate neighbors.

On another level it can be seen in the way in which each individual isolates himself from other individuals. Modern men and women rarely touch each other in public. Individual relationships are governed by complex rituals that mitigate against any real recognition of the existence of another human being. The complex etiquette of telephone conversations between two businessmen is one example of this. Two secretaries vie with each other to put the other boss on the line first and thus establish the greater status of their own boss. Neither the secretaries nor their bosses communicate their own feelings and personality to each other.

Additionally, sex has become mechanical and women have been placed more and more in the role of an object. Any issue of *Playboy* magazine epitomizes this trend.

In each of our roles we play a narrowly defined part that does not overlap with other people and does not provide any contact—physical, emotional, or mental—with other people. We have become separate islands while mouthing the old formulas of contact and community.

Man alienated from his work

Man is alienated from his work because of the mechanical nature of most jobs today. Man has become an extension of a machine or a machine himself. There are very few jobs that accept or encourage creativity. There are very few positions that can be thought of as vocations or careers that individuals would dedicate themselves to for anything other than status or money. There is no community among workers except the common bond of unhappiness in the job and complaints about the work. Listening to almost any group of colleagues in any business or profession, you hear complaints solely about their working life. No one is happy on the job.

Money and status are the only rewards that we consider in career choices. We do not consider what the effect of our life will be on ourselves or our families or our communities. We consider ourselves successful and "fulfilled" if we make more money or have more status than our neighbors, and then we spend our lives complaining about the work that we do and the conditions in which we work. But we almost never take the next step of attempting to do something about it. We rarely if ever attempt to modify the conditions of our lives.

We are so alienated from ourselves, others, and our work that meaningful change seems impossible. We are, to use Charles

Reich's word, overwhelmed by our "powerlessness." Alienation is not rooted in a single cause for all men and women. Each person has a different combination of causes operating on and in him. Therefore each individual will see the solution from a slightly different perspective, if, in fact, he is aware of his alienation at all. Even if I am not always aware that I am sick, this does not actually change the fact of the disease within me. I may catch glimpses of my problems from time to time without identifying them clearly, but that does not change the existence of the problems.

The basic problem is one of awareness. The existentialists first stressed the necessity of being fully aware of the human condition, and one would think that the constant flood of books, articles, and television programs that deal with the deteriorating conditions of modern life would produce some sort of response, but it seems that no one is listening, or if they listen they do not recognize a personal application.

Here again the existentialists made an important point. Awareness does not come often, and it is usually produced by some unusual situation in which an individual is forced to recognize some of the realities of life. The existentialist approach, although it suggested the main themes that the New Left is working out, was essentially elitist. The New Left does not agree that it is impossible for large numbers to become aware (though it admits that it may be unlikely). An excellent example of this point appeared in *Avatar*. ". . . it's a world of sleep-walkers," but some, a few, are beginning to wake up—"and not many are going to awaken but those who will awaken will awaken fully . . . ."[4]

The New Left operates on the assumption, however, that it *is* possible for most people to recognize their condition and to overcome it, at least to some degree. They believe that it is easier for

---

[4] Eben Given, "The Wakening of the People," *Avatar*, September 1, 1967, reprinted in Jesse Kornbluth (ed.), *Notes from the New Underground; An Anthology* (New York: The Viking Press, 1968), p. 27.

the young, who are thought to be, and in some cases probably are, more flexible than the "over 30" generation, but they act on the assumption that it is possible for everyone.

Action

The basic solution is action. As we noted earlier, both the existentialists and the New Left put a premium on action.[5] The existentialist argued that an individual created his own values and his own meaning through his actions. In other words, you know a man through his deeds rather than his words.

This also means that you are what you do rather than what you say you are, and action rather than words as the means of defining an individual and revealing his character has an honorable past in Western thought. It can be found in early Greek and Hebrew thought and in almost every period up to the present, but until its recent revival it was neglected in the recent past.

Here we find the basis of the most common New Left criticism of contemporary society—hypocrisy. We use fine words such as "peace," "freedom," and "justice," and we create ghettos and slums, and we hate and kill. We seem to really say, "Do what I say, not what I do"—actually, what is really being said is, "Do what I do, not what I say." In any case, we lie to ourselves and to our children. Hypocrisy is one more symptom of alienation. It reflects a separation between word and deed, and it demonstrates our alienation from ourselves as we say one thing and do another. The adage "Don't let your left hand know what your right hand is doing" is simply another example. It encourages doing and saying inconsistent things. And the existentialist and the New Left respond that you are what you do—what you say is irrele-

---

[5] In *The Making of a Counter Culture; Reflections on the Technocratic Society and Its Youthful Opposition* (Garden City, N.Y.: Doubleday & Co., 1969), Chapter 2, Theodore Roszak discusses the tendency to anti-intellectualism in the New Left and points to some of the dangers of such an approach. Finally, he suggests alternatively the danger of an overly intellectual approach. Although he oversimplifies the problem a bit, his discussion is well worth reading.

vant, a series of well-meaning but essentially dishonest platitudes.

The basic theme of the New Left is the stress on action—you are defined by your deeds. This provides a step in the direction of a rediscovery of meaning and of self, but it is different from a meaning or a definition of self that is provided by religion or ideology. It is a meaning and a definition that is created by the individual. If you accept that you are what you do, you must attempt to behave in such a way that you are comfortable with yourself.

Creation of self

In the discussion of alienation, a theme that kept reappearing as an aspect of alienated life was the lack of creativity, the lack of a creative component in everyday life. And in the answer to alienation we come back to the essential need to create, and to create on the most basic level, the level of self.

We can see the expressions of the need to create all around us every day. The worker who spends his off hours tinkering with an old car is a creative artist.[6] The suburbanite in his garden or his basement workship is a creative artist. Both are trying to return to an older craft tradition that jobs no longer provide. But what they are trying to do is impossible. With the exception of the custom car builder, who is a sculptor, and a few others, the traditional creative outlets have become dominated by technology and are of little help. The gardener and the basement craftsman invest huge sums in equipment to make the job easier, but they merely succeed in cutting themselves off from what they want to achieve.[7]

The need to work with the hands is at least a reflection of·a deeper need to overcome alienation, but the old car, the basement

---

[6] For the extent of this phenomenon, see the title essay of Tom Wolfe's *Kandy-Kolored Tangerine-Flake Streamline Baby* (New York: Pocket Books, 1965), pp. 62–89.

[7] Of course consciously the gardener and the basement craftsman may be trying to escape from a nagging wife and screaming children, and that may be all there is to it. Also, it *is* possible that at least a few men simply enjoy the garden or the workshop.

workshop, and the garden only fill a very small part of life. There are still the hours of boredom and drudgery on the job. The unhappy marriage and the uncongenial family still exist. The avocation is at most a temporary respite.

Can most men and women escape permanently from their barren lives while still remaining sane and alive? The New Left argues that it is possible, although difficult. How? By thorough self-awareness and honesty. By a recognition of the social and psychic forces at work upon us. By overcoming the false needs engendered by technocratic society. By creating out of this new awareness and honesty, a new person that is authentic.

First, one of the dominant characteristics of the Movement is an intense introspection, of both individuals and groups. There is a constant attempt to reach honesty with oneself and with others. Although this attempt is sometimes carried to extremes, the point of attempting it is important. "Know Thyself" is the first rule. Of course it is assumed it is possible to know ourselves, and this gives rise to the popularity of psychological theories on the New Left and in society. During the '50s and early '60s, individual psychoanalysis was popular. This has given way to group therapy, and for the New Left group therapy has completely replaced individual psychoanalysis. But although the change is immensely significant in that the whole movement has become community-rather than individual-oriented, the underlying concern with psychic states and levels of awareness represented by both approaches remains the same.

This attitude is reflected in a variety of ways. Most prominently in:

1. The brief popularity among many groups of the writings of Norman O. Brown.[8]

---

[8] Brown's popularity is not of major significance to the topic at hand, but he does deal with many similar themes. For a brief discussion and critique of Brown see Roszak, op. cit., chap. 3.

2. The resurgence of religion on the New Left.

3. The drug culture.

Points two and three are interesting commentaries on the anti-intellectual side of the New Left and are intimately related since many religious themes are tied into parts of the drug culture.[9] But fortunately for both the drug culture and the religious upsurge on the New Left, they are not identical.

In the late '50s and early '60s, Zen first became popular in this country, particularly among the Beatniks. Kerouac's *The Dharma Bums* (1958) may not have been the first novel of Zen, but it helped to make it popular. Gary Snyder, the real name of the hero of *The Dharma Bums,* Alan Watts, and D. T. Suzuki (in ascending order of sophistication) were, and still are, widely read. Although the level of sophistication among Zen devotees was, and is, not high, an effort was made to comprehend this simple-complex nonreligion.[10] This was the first major turn to the East among contemporary Western youth, and the appeal of the East has continued.

Specifically, the interest in Zen has continued, but it has been added to and partially supplanted by an interest in Hinduism. This shift has produced a wide variety of groups that copy one or

----

[9] See, for example, Timothy Leary, *High Priest* (New York: World, 1968).

[10] There is clearly insufficient space here to adequately characterize Zen Buddhism, but I shall list a few major characteristics and a few sources for further study. Zen is anti-intellectual (study will not bring one to truths; it is more likely to get in the way). Zen includes meditation but not worship—there is no god or anything equivalent to god. Zen is life-confirming —the joys of the flesh are good, but they should be enjoyed moderately. The "goal" of Zen is *satori* (enlightenment), which is, much oversimplified, the recognition of the oneness of the universe—the individual but a minute part of the cosmos and at the same time all of the cosmos. The interested reader should consult, for introductions, D. T. Suzuki, *Zen Buddhism,* ed. William Barrett (Garden City, N.Y.: Doubleday, 1956); Alan Watts, *The Way of Zen* (New York: New American Library, 1957); and Watts, *Beat Zen, Square Zen and Zen* (San Francisco: City Lights Books, 1959).

more of the Hindu sects. Philosophically Hinduism and Zen have basic affinities, but Hinduism, and particularly those parts taken up in this country, emphasizes ritual much more than Zen.[11]

Generally the upsurge of religion on the New Left has been part of the search for self. And it has turned to the East because Oriental religion has always stressed awareness of self, consciousness, and mysticism, whereas Western religion has always been a bit suspicious of its mystics.[12]

One may wonder if the interest in religion does not reflect a fairly simple approach to the creation of an authentic self—the acceptance of an image of self from the religion or the creation of a self in the image of the religion. But even if it is an easy way to selfhood, it still reflects the search. On the other hand, the approach through religion may not be simple. Eastern religion is not easily understood by most Westerners, and success in achieving the goals of the religions is even harder. The person who is simply searching for an easy route to self-awareness will probably leave rapidly. Long hours of meditation; a simple, and usually vegetarian, diet; and the struggle to understand the complexity of the religion will test the sincerity of most fairly rapidly. Those who stay will probably be serious, and they may find what they are looking for. Even if the search through religion is not the same search that most of the New Left have in mind, it is a closely parallel phenomenon.

It is contended by some that the drug culture is essentially the

---

11 Hinduism, which is made up of many different sects, is too complex to adequately summarize.

The interested reader should see William Theodore de Bary et al. (comps.), *Sources of Indian Tradition* (New York: Columbia University Press, 1958), particularly Part Three; Sarvepalli Radhakrishnan and Charles A. Moore (eds.), *A Source Book of Indian Philosophy* (Princeton, N.J.: Princeton University Press, 1957); and Heinrich Zimmer, *Philosophies of India,* ed. Joseph Campbell (New York: Meridian Books, Inc., 1956).

12 Along this line there has been a growth of Christian sects, usually mystic, but sometimes even fundamentalist, in addition to the interest in the East.

same phenomenon.[13] The drug culture fulfills a number of functions for the New Left.

1. It is an avenue in the search for the authentic self. Some see it as providing the only such avenue.
2. It is a symbol of the unity of the New Left and its differences from the Establishment.
3. It is a symbol of the attack of the Establishment on the New Left and the main avenue of the attack.

For our purposes, the first point is the only one of interest, and all that needs to be said in this context is that drugs act in the same way as the Oriental religions as a means of opening the mind to new states of awareness and a route to a new self.

But the drug culture and the New Left are not identical. It can probably be argued that most members of the Movement smoke marijuana and have tried LSD or one of the other psychedelics, but this does not make them part of the drug culture. The drug culture focuses on the drug experience. Its social and political content is very limited. The passing of the joint or the cup with the drug in it may form a small community for awhile, but one that breaks up rapidly, and there is little concern with social and political questions beyond the drug laws. This is not true of all members of the drug culture, but it is true of most of them, and it clearly distinguishes the New Left from the drug culture.

Acceptance of self

The creation of self, having been treated under three headings —creation by action, religion, and drugs—can now give way to the final, and most prevalent approach to the search for authenticity—the identification and acceptance of self. There are basic similarities between this approach and the former approaches, but there are significant differences also.

---

[13] Roszak in his discussion of the drug culture is so upset by it that he misses the whole point. For all its excesses and dangers, which he effectively points out, the drug culture is part of the search for an authentic self.

The major similarity is in the need for awareness. An individual trying to identify his authentic being must be constantly aware of his feelings and motivations. This can lead to an intense introspection, but most often this is avoided. The individual is expected to identify himself through interaction with others going through the same process—hence the popularity of group therapy and sensitivity training. As a person becomes increasingly aware of himself and others, he has achieved a major step toward the identification of self.

The New Left says, "Do your own thing," but an individual must find himself and his thing before he can do it. Therefore there is a deep concern with and emphasis on the search for each individual's identity. Communes and other groups spend much time and effort in helping their members find themselves. Sometimes the process is one of mutual support and sympathy; sometimes it is one of mutual criticism and ego destruction.

The individual must find and assert himself and his thing, but he must avoid the "ego trip." Individualism does not mean egotism. Your thing is not better than someone else's thing; it is merely different. Thus your search and discovery should not make you look down on others. Each person with all his or her separate peculiarities is equally valuable. Finding yourself asserts the value of each person; it does not place one above another.

This process is particularly prevalent and important in the women's groups. Women have been so completely objectified by society that they have come to accept object roles and not to expect to be thought of as individual human beings. The woman's movement is a major step toward an individual woman finding value and selfhood within herself rather than as an adjunct to someone else.[14]

Here is the perfect example of the search for authenticity. A woman, brought up to believe that certain roles and attitudes are the only ones for women, discovers that they aren't the ones she

---

[14] The women's movement will be treated more extensively in Chapter 4.

wants. She faces a basic conflict between what she knows is best for her and what she has internalized through years of training (indoctrination). There is no easy answer. She cannot simply say I choose this role or that without conflict with either her mature interests or her training. She must struggle to find herself and if the choice conflicts with society's expectations for women she will have to face discrimination and ridicule. A contemporary man's search and struggle is merely a pale reflection of what a contemporary woman must go through.[15]

The problems that women face today are illustrative of the problems faced by many, even if not in quite such an acute form. Basically each of us either accepts some combination of roles that is forced on us by society, or we search out a combination of roles that uniquely expresses our personality. The latter approach identifies and accepts your authentic self, and taking it leads to one major characteristic of the New Left that may not be immediately apparent—the recognition, acceptance, and even the encouragement of individual differences. The New Left's concern with and emphasis on the group and a sense of community does not mean the loss of the individual.

---

[15] Of course there are parallel problems for the black man (and doubly so for the black woman), and for the homosexual.

3

"DO YOUR OWN THING"

The phrase "Do your own thing" is a concise and apt description of the meaning of freedom for the New Left. It is closely related to the search for the authentic self in that in order to "do your own thing" you have to first be able to find it. And to be able to find it means that the avenues of the search must be open to use. And, of course, once having found your thing, you must also be able to practice it. Hence, freedom for the New Left relates first to the search for the authentic self and second to the ability to be yourself. The New Left, though, would not make the analytical distinction I have just made because they see the search, discovery, and practice as one ongoing activity.

But while freedom is one of the central concepts of New Left thought, it is also one of the central problems. The street maxim that goes "Your freedom to swing your arm stops at the end of my nose" illustrates the basic problem of freedom—one person's freedom always involves another person's; that is, any exercise of freedom is always limited by the needs and freedoms of others. In its insistence on the importance of community and equality in addition to freedom, the New Left clearly recognizes this limitation. We all act within groupings, and we are limited in the range of our actions by the other people involved. But, as the New Left points out, our potential for action is greatly expanded through interaction with other people, particularly in a close-knit community.

But freedom is an even more complex notion. There is another maxim which says, "Liberty is the freedom to do what you want as long as you do not harm someone else" and of course "harm" is defined differently at different periods of time. The current controversy over pollution is one example of how the definition changes. For more than a century we collectively polluted the environment—but we did not think of our actions as harmful; today we do.

Also, harm is not a simple idea. There is, for example, the simplistic admonition that generations of mothers have given their children who do not eat their vegetables: "Think of the starving children in _____" (fill in whatever country or continent your mother told you). Obviously this harm is far removed from our daily lives, and the argument certainly failed with most children. But it provides us with an example that we can use for analyzing the meaning of freedom. Freedom involves an actor, an action (this can include thought or belief), and an effect or result in a setting or environment. In the example just given, the child is the actor, the action is eating or refusing to eat the vegetables, and the effect is the supposed harm on the starving children in _____. Obviously the notion of harm posed by the mother is meaningless; whether or not her child eats the vegetables has no effect on the starving children in _____.

But even though the admonition is weak in force, and probably refers more to the child's luck in being born in a place where vegetables are available, the example still represents freedom. It involves choice between two actions, eating or not eating. And it involves an effect, such as the good done to the body by vegetables, not getting dessert, or getting spanked. Thus, freedom involves choices between alternative actions with one or more possible effects or results. Given complete information, choice may be fairly simple, but most choices must be made without complete information regarding either alternatives or results.

And there is the setting. So far I have looked at freedom from the point of view of the single actor and have ignored the problem of the setting. But in the question of freedom in social and political thought, the setting is all-important because it is only within a specific setting that it is possible to talk about free or unfree acts.

Each setting, society, or culture produces a somewhat different complex of acceptable alternatives and desired results. The degree to which the range of choice is limited in a particular setting is the degree of freedom in that setting. The limitation can be direct, such as through law, or indirect, such as through custom or socialization. In either case, the complex of limitations, overt and covert, produces the degree of freedom in that setting. Diversity may be encouraged or discouraged and freedom may be thought of as a condition in which diverse alternatives are available to the actor. To the degree that a society encourages or accepts diversity, it is free; to the degree it does not, it is not. Put more negatively and conventionally, freedom entails the ability of an individual or group of individuals to act (thought, speech, movement, and so forth) within specified or at least specifiable limitations.

But it is impossible to stop here. Freedom, it will be recalled, always involves the needs and freedom of others. The central problem of freedom is the balancing of differing claims. The New Left believes that this balancing can best be achieved in a close-knit egalitarian community. The traditional democratic approach to the problem is to use law to specify the limits of action of both citizenry and government, and to provide means for the orderly change of priorities. The New Left, of course, believes that this approach has failed.

The New Left critique

The New Left position regarding contemporary society is primarily that the limitations are too strict. "Using all the means at its disposal, the existing System strives to prevent us from introducing those conditions in which men can live creative lives without war, hunger, and repressive work."[1] The implications of

---

[1] Rudi Dutschke, "On Anti-authoritarianism," in Carl Oglesby (ed.), *The New Left Reader* (New York: Grove Press, 1969), p. 244.

this statement for the positive aspects of New Left thought are very significant and will be developed shortly, but let us look at the critical implications first.

The focus of the criticism is "the System," which means capitalism, the military-industrial complex, and government. More specifically this means that the legal system and the work situation[2] are repressive and the educational system is particularly repressive.[3] In fact all existing economic, social, and political institutions are considered repressive.

It is somewhat more difficult to specify the precise mechanisms of repression and the effects of repression on the individual, but some of each can be sketched and since the mechanisms and the effects are closely related, the same sketch can serve for both. The most significant point that the New Left sees is the socialization process—the attempt to mold people so that they will believe themselves to be happy doing what the system needs them to do: produce and consume unnecessary products. Each individual is a potential worker and consumer. Whether he or she works on an assembly line, shuffles paper in a large office, types, or does unpaid domestic labor, he or she produces and/or consumes so that the production-consumption cycle may continue. People are a necessary cog in the machine.[4]

---

[2] See, for example, Charles Denby, "Workers Battle Automation," in Priscilla Long (ed.), *The New Left: A Collection of Essays* (Boston: Porter Sargent, 1969), pp. 151–71.

[3] The New Left literature on this topic is immense. Here are a few fairly representative examples: Noam Chomsky, "Knowledge and Power: Intellectuals and the Welfare-Warfare State," in Long (ed.), pp. 172–99; Part III, "Campus Agonistes: The Student Rebels," in Leo Hamalian and Frederick R. Karl (eds.), *The Radical Vision: Essays for the Seventies* (New York: Thomas Y. Crowell Co., 1970), pp. 169–255; the section entitled "New Politics and the University," in Harold Jaffe and John Tytell (eds.), *The American Experience: A Radical Reader* (New York: Harper and Row, 1970), pp. 115–202; and the section entitled "High School Women: Three Views," in Robin Morgan (ed.), *Sisterhood Is Powerful. An Anthology of Writings from the Women's Liberation Movement* (New York: Random House, 1970), pp. 362–75.

[4] In a brilliant satire entitled "The Midas Plague" (1954), Frederick

But the individual must be content doing this or he will make an inadequate worker and consumer. Thus, the argument goes, he is molded from youth to take his "proper" place in society. He is taught to believe that having material possessions means that he has achieved success and the good life. At the same time, since a pool of unskilled labor is needed, some are condemned to perpetual poverty. Racism is the means by which this is made acceptable to the masses. Since more consumers are needed than producers, sexism is used to keep women at home consuming or in poorly paid menial jobs.

Racism, sexism, and poverty are the most obvious examples of limitations that have been accepted, ignored, or defended for centuries. All three constitute clear denials of liberty. The first two confine large parts of the population to a second-class status through poor education (even for the best educated), degrading day-to-day treatment, and, most significantly, by being taught that they are inferior.

Poverty is very similar to racism and sexism in its effects—poor education, degrading existence, belief in one's own inferiority. It is also similar to sexism in that its effects are only now being recognized and are not generally known or accepted as being true. The effects of racism have been known a little longer and are a little more widely accepted as being true.

Like racism and sexism, poverty has a cumulative effect on future generations. The longer its effects are felt, the harder it is to break out. The blatant examples that can be seen of the effects of the system denying liberty to large parts of the population point to the validity of part of the New Left critique.

Molding is clearly the most basic kind of repression, but there are others. On one level there is the educational system that presents a false picture of history and the world by leaving out black history, women's history, the history of radicalism, and so forth,

---

Pohl pictured a society in which the poor were required to consume vast quantities each month while the rich could consume less. See it in *The Case Against Tomorrow* (New York: Ballantine, 1957).

and by teaching only what is good about the United States and only what is bad about the rest of the world. Although much education is not really this bad, and lip service is paid to breadth and objectivity, the emphasis produces the distortion.

On another level, there is the overt political repression of dissent that does not accept or follow the rules of the game. Hence there is repression of those for whom the rules are wrong and those for whom reform is too slow. This takes the form of the legal denial of rights of speech, assembly, and press, the harassment of individuals and groups through the strict enforcement of laws that are not enforced for others, and, of course, violence.

The system creates a limited man, and if he comes to act freely, he is suppressed. This is the New Left view of liberty in contemporary society. We are molded and formed until we, our authentic selves, are destroyed or lost. Creativity is destroyed because it is unnecessary. Love is lost. All this because the system needs producers and consumers. Although they are clearly not of the New Left, the picture is similar to that found in Aldous Huxley's *Brave New World* (1932) or Eugene Zamiatin's *We* (1924). Happiness through material possessions (and promiscuity) is bought at the price of freedom. The choice is happiness or freedom and the system has chosen happiness. The New Left demands freedom.[5]

The New Left concept

The basic idea of liberty for the New Left is expressed by and encompassed in the phrase that serves as the title of this chapter: "Do your own thing." This is an answer to repression. Most specifically, it is a response to molding an individual into a producer and consumer.

"Do your own thing" is an answer in that it relates directly to

---

[5] This theme is of considerable importance in Western thought. See the essay entitled "The Fear of Utopia," in Robert C. Elliott, *The Shape of Utopia: Studies in a Literary Genre* (Chicago: The University of Chicago Press, 1970), pp. 84–101, in which he traces the themes of *Brave New World* and *We* back to the Grand Inquisitor tale in Dostoevski's *The Brothers Karamozov* (1880).

the search for the authentic self. It is impossible to "do your own thing" until you have discovered what it is. Once it has been discovered, there should be no limit on practicing it. Therefore there are two parts to freedom: (1) the essential freedom of search and discovery, and (2) the freedom to practice "your own thing" after the discovery of it. Again, it should be noted that the analytical distinction between search and discovery is not made by the New Left. For them the process is one of ongoing search or continual discovery.

A variety of life styles, a variety of psychic states discovered either through religion or drugs, and widely diverse styles of dress are often expressions of the search. Thus, the search cannot take place without the ability to freely adopt different styles and attitudes. Any limitation on the life style, the taking of drugs, or the style of clothes can be seen as a limitation on the search.

Such limitations may not seem particularly important on the surface, but they take on symbolic importance to the one who is limited. Long hair, drugs, and so forth are badges of belonging, direct attacks on the limitations the system wants to impose, and a very important part of the search. Alcohol and tobacco have bad effects on the body and are allowed, protected, and supported by the system. The bad effects of marijuana are not as well established as those of alcohol and tobacco, but marijuana is systematically suppressed. This is seen, probably rightly, as an attack on a life style rather than an attack on drug abuse.

The individual must be free to find himself. In the process he may harm himself, but he must have that freedom. Past experience in life styles is not readily transferrable; each individual must taste a variety of such styles before he finds that combination that suits him best, and that combination is likely to change over time so that the search will be continuous. The most difficult time, though, is at the beginning and some communes have attempted to serve as stopping-off and starting places for those who have dropped out.

The search and discovery are continuous and thus freedom

must extend beyond the period of youth or adolescence which traditionally has been accepted as a period in which an individual can be expected to do many things that would not be accepted in an adult. This was simply the recognition that this is a time of searching and of relative freedom before the work and family experience. But this tolerance of life styles must be extended from youth through adulthood. In the past an occasional eccentric was accepted. This is no longer sufficient. Communities holding radically divergent life styles must be both accepted and encouraged.

The tremendous diversity among individuals must be recognized and communities must be formed that will accept and encourage these differences. The community situation can give the individual the security and freedom to find and practice their own styles of life. In addition, there can be a wide variety of living situations and styles available to experiment with and live in if they represent the individual's needs and desires.

The basic notion is a simple one. Society must be organized so that freedom and diversity are accepted and encouraged. The specific structure is that of the community organization. But there will always be conflict between the needs and desires of the individual and the community and among individuals. These conflicts may be minimized by the communal ideal of the New Left but even there they will not disappear.

Each Dropper is free. Each does what he wants. No rules, no duties, no obligations. Anarchy. But as anarchistic as the growth of an organism which has its own internal needs and fulfills them in a natural, simple way, without compulsion.[6]

This image is about as close to complete freedom as is possible. Internally self-directed cooperating individuals living together in a commune may be able to function without rules, but the gen-

---

[6] Albin Wagner, "Drop City: A Total Living Environment," *Avatar*, August 4, 1967, quoted in Jesse Kornbluth (ed.), *Notes from the New Underground: An Anthology* (New York: The Viking Press, 1968), p. 233.

eral experience is that admonishment and reminder is needed even if rules (laws) are unnecessary.

But even if freedom of this degree is obtainable, it is only rarely so now. Much of the New Left has focused on developing alternative institutions that are freer than the institutions of contemporary society. The free school movement is an excellent example. Individuals take what they want. Individuals teach what they want. Classes are taught on a wide range of subjects. The distinction between teacher and student is broken down in most, although not all, of the classes. People come together to share their knowledge and learn from each other rather than being fairly passive receptacles of a presentation by a teacher. These alternative institutions are beginning little by little to provide possibilities for greater freedom within the context of contemporary society, but it is a difficult process.

One of the most basic problems within any community, but particularly one based on a belief in an authentic self, is the possible conflict between majority and minority opinions. If the community attempts to reach decisions through consensus, this may not be a problem if the people actually respect each other. But if there is a sizeable majority, an individual must be very sure of himself to withstand the pressure of opinion. Opinion may be one of the greatest dangers to freedom for the free community. For the system to work, people must be willing to suspend judgment on or simply not judge other people or not express their negative feelings overtly. The commune must be mutually supportive and positive to allow freedom.

In addition, it has been argued that the achievement of equality will limit freedom. On the one hand, there is the argument that any attempt at treating different people in the same way has to infringe freedom. On the other hand, the basic position of the New Left is that equality and freedom are not only compatible but complementary. Looked at from the perspective of the poor, the minorities, and women, the point is self-evident. Looked at from the perspective of the rich, the majority, and the male, the point is less evident, but is still made. Everyone is suppressed by such inequalities. Only with greater equality will anyone be free to discover themselves and live the lives they wish. Hence, equality and liberty should be seen as complementary, rather than opposed to each other. Differences are good but only within an egalitarian society can these differences be truly and fully expressed. Freedom is only meaningful in an egalitarian society, and equality is only meaningful with freedom.

The relationship between equality and liberty is an important theme in the thought of the New Left, and the relationship provides one of the themes of the following chapters. The compatibility of the two concepts is a basic axiom of New Left thought and in the following chapters, particularly in the next two, a variety of the New Left's attempts to clarify the relationship and work it out in practice will be presented. The first, the attempt to clarify the relationship, can be seen most clearly in the re-definition of equality. The second, the attempt to work out the relationship in practice can be seen most clearly in the central concept of community. For the New Left this is the most important part.

And it is in the community that the conflict between individual needs and individual freedoms and the solution to these conflicts can be seen best. The New Left sees the tight-knit community operating on the basis of participatory democracy as the best guarantee of freedom and equality.

4
COMMUNITY

Everybody talks about community, but nobody defines it.[1] Admittedly, the concept is a difficult one to define with any real clarity, and this is particularly true in connection with radical thought. Therefore, in order to help clarify the concept, two recent attempts to define the term will be noted.

... community is both empirically descriptive of a social structure and normatively toned. It refers both to the unit of a society as it is and to the aspects of the unit that are valued if they exist, desired in their absence. Community is indivisible from human actions, purposes, and values. It expresses our vague yearnings for a commonality of desire, a communion with those around us, an extension of the bonds of kin and friend to all those who share a common fate with us.[2]

The very vagueness of this description is one of its most important characteristics. The language does not seem to express adequately the interrelationships the authors have in mind. Therefore they are forced to speak of "vague yearnings" and the like.

---

[1] Or alternatively, everybody defines it. George A. Hillery, Jr., has identified 94 definitions in his "Definitions of Community: Areas of Agreement," *Rural Sociology*, 20 (June, 1955), pp. 111–23. René König comments that Hillery's list is incomplete. See his *The Community*, trans. by Edward Fitzgerald (London: Routledge & Kegan Paul Ltd., 1968), p. 22.

[2] David W. Minar and Scott Greer, "Introduction," *The Concept of Community: Readings with Interpretations* (Chicago: Aldine Publishing Co., 1969), p. ix.

As should be fairly obvious, the word shares its derivation with "common," and the authors use *common, commonality,* and *communion* in characterizing it. Since all the members of a community may have in common could be merely the membership in the community, it is necessary to go further.

By community I mean something that goes far beyond mere local community. The word, as we find it in much nineteenth- and twentieth-century thought, encompasses all forms of relationships which are characterized by a high degree of personal intimacy, emotional depth, moral commitment, social cohesion, and continuity in time. Community is founded on man conceived in his wholeness rather than in one or another of the roles, taken separately, that he may hold in a social order. It draws its psychological strength from levels of motivation deeper than those of mere volition or interest, and it achieves its fulfillment in a submergence of individual will that is not possible in unions of mere convenience or rational assent. Community is a fusion of feeling and thought, of tradition and commitment, of membership and volition.[3]

It is now possible to see that community refers to groups, a member of which shares, in addition to mere group membership, some degree of personal intimacy with the other members of the group. The higher the degree of personal intimacy, and the closer the group comes to the sort of relationship that is supposed to exist in the close-knit family,[4] the more truly is it a community.

It is unlikely, though, that each individual in a community, however small and close-knit it may be, will have the same type of relationship with each of the other individuals. And the larger the community the less likely this becomes. Hence, a community will have at least two types of relationships within it—the close, intimate ties and the indirect, acquaintanceship ties.

Nisbet's characterization of the concept of community designates the personal elements that are so important, while remain-

---

[3] Robert A. Nisbet, *The Sociological Tradition* (New York: Basic Books, Inc., Publishers, 1966), pp. 47–8.

[4] Shortly we will look at notions of community that go well beyond the ties of, for example, marriage.

ing vague enough about the other elements to avoid being over-limiting. Therefore, it is possible to turn from community as a general ideal of Western culture to the New Left critique of the institutions of society as they relate to community.

The New Left critique

The New Left critique of community in contemporary society may be simply summarized in this statement: "There isn't any." A discussion of the details of the critique would be unduly repetitious because although there are differences in the various statements made by the New Left writers, their conclusions are all the same.

Additionally, the New Left critique is not essentially different from the Old Left or the far right critique. The only differences that can be found among the various approaches are found in the different causes given for the lack of community. These differences do, to some extent, reflect the differences among the various groups, so it will be worthwhile to look briefly at the causes given by the New Left.

The basic analysis, as given in the three major works that deal with the problem, Charles A. Reich's *The Greening of America* (1970), Theodore Roszak's *The Making of a Counter Culture* (1969), and Philip Slater's *The Pursuit of Loneliness* (1970), is that American culture has been so dominated by the competitiveness of the market economy that it has lost all possibility of close interpersonal relationships, at least as long as the competitiveness remains.

This analysis is essentially the same as the Marxist analysis, with the exception that it removes the class distinctions that Marxist commentators generally include. One could add many other points to the analysis, such as our tremendous geographical mobility or the destruction of neighborhoods through urban "renewal" and suburbanization, but while some of the authors deal with these phenomena, the basic analysis lays the blame on the competitiveness fostered by our economic system.

The critique then continues and argues that this competitiveness is unnecessary, is no longer required, and finally, that the economic system needs a major overhaul.[5] Again, this part of the critique is not peculiar to the New Left.

Before turning to the New Left alternative, however, let's look a bit more at the critique. Slater deals with the question most directly. He puts it as follows:

We seek a private house, a private means of transportation, a private laundry, self-service stores, and do-it-yourself skills of every kind. An enormous technology seems to have set itself the task of making it unnecessary for one human being ever to ask anything of another in the course of going about his daily business. Even within the family Americans are unique in this feeling that each member should have a separate room, and even a separate telephone, television, and car, when economically possible. We seek more and more privacy, and feel more and more alienated and lonely when we get it.[6]

Here we see some of the causes the New Left assigns to alienation. Although Slater represents the most intellectual side of New Left thought, his comments on this point are fairly representative of New Left thinking as a whole. Movement thought is coming more and more to focus on alienation and the breakdown of community as the major faults of contemporary life. It is contended that we have become isolated automatons following patterns determined by and more appropriate to machines. In other words, we have become machines.

And we have come to need and search for isolation from our fellow man rather than communion with him. And the more we cut ourselves off, the more we lose the possibility of understanding ourselves or others, the harder it will be ever to be close to another human being. The New Left is arguing against too great a stress on the individual if it cuts people off from each other. It is

---

[5] See, for example, Dave Gilbert, "Consumption: Domestic Imperialism," in Long (ed.), op. cit., pp. 26–42.

[6] Philip E. Slater, *The Pursuit of Loneliness; American Culture at the Breaking Point* (Boston: Beacon Press, 1970), p. 7.

saying that we have destroyed all sense of community and that we must work to rebuild it.

The New Left concept of community

The New Left concept of community basically repeats the general concept as we have defined it, but with a few significant additions. Before turning to these additions or extensions of the concept, let us first look at the way in which community is supposed to solve the problem noted in the previous section.

Essentially the problem has two parts: (1) competitiveness, and (2) alienation. The development of a feeling of community is a direct solution to alienation. An individual who is an integral part of a community should not feel alienated. He should not be alienated from others because, if he were, he would not be an integral member of the community.[7] Although solving one of the elements of alienation does not necessarily entail the solution of the other elements, it is usually argued by the New Left that the solutions are related to community.

The alienation of the individual from himself should be taken care of by the atmosphere provided by a community—security, freedom, and acceptance. And the alienation of the individual from his work should at least be partially solved by the same factors. The community might be able to provide a work atmosphere that would help overcome alienation. And, if an individual is no longer alienated from himself and others, the rest of his life is likely to be improved also.[8]

Overcoming competitiveness is part of the process of overcoming alienation and a result of it. Competitiveness is a cause of alienation in the sense that it separates an individual from other

---

[7] This is one of the points in Abbie Hoffman's *Woodstock Nation; A Talk-Rock Album* (New York: Vintage Books, 1969).

[8] Fredy Perlman, in "The Reproduction of Daily Life," in Arthur Lothstein (ed.), *"All We Are Saying . . .": The Philosophy of the New Left* (New York: Capricorn Books, 1970), pp. 133–54, makes this point in the context of an interesting analysis of the alienating qualities of capitalism.

individuals. To a competitor, others are seen as opponents to be defeated. Of course there are varying degrees of this feeling. In many sports, competition is supposedly limited to the playing field and by "the rules of the game." In business the rules are more flexible and the game may extend to all of life. In education, the competition for grades encourages lying and cheating as well as the greater effort it supposedly encourages.

As a result of alienation, competition is seen as the only possible route for one already cut off from others. The nonalienated would find the division of people into opposing groups strange and uncomfortable. This of course does not include the temporary competition of most sports, particularly those emphasizing either individual skill or the finely tuned coordination of a team. Hence, community is seen as a major part of the solution to the problems we face today.

But we still have to look carefully at the extensions or additions that the New Left have put onto the basic concept. The first point of addition or extension is a very general one and concerns the degree of closeness involved in the community. In talking about the general definition of community at the beginning of this chapter, I said that it involved close interpersonal relations among some members of the group. The New Left ideal is very close interpersonal relations among all members of the group. As Norman O. Brown put it, "Apocalypse is the dissolution of group as numerical series, as in representative democracy, and its replacement by the group as fusion, as communion."[9] Or as Gary Snyder put it, "The Great Subculture . . . transmits a community style of life, with an ecstatically positive vision of spiritual and physical love . . ."[10] Both of these statements indicate that the new community is seen as tightly woven. The members are close to the

---

[9] Norman O. Brown, *Love's Body* (New York: Random House, 1966), p. 255.

[10] Gary Snyder, "Why Tribe," *Earth House Hold*, reprinted in Harold Jaffe and John Tytell (eds.), p. 259.

image of the loving family, or, most appropriately, some of the idealized pictures we have of tribal life—a close-knit group that is capable of sharing everything and excluding no one.

The tribal image is only a good one if idealized, because traditionally tribes often, but not always, had a rigid authority system with age, up to a certain point, the major basis for authority. Also, the tribes found in any given area varied tremendously in their social systems. Therefore, its major value is as an image, however idealized, of a community group that approached the desired closeness.

Whether it is called a family, a tribe, or a commune is unimportant as long as the meaning is clear—a new degree of closeness in a group. One symbol of this degree of closeness and a real manifestation of it is found in group sex. The major expressions of the ideas involved have been literary, particularly in Robert Heinlein's *Stranger in a Strange Land* (1961) and Robert Rimmer's *Harrad Experiment* (1966) and *Proposition 31* (1968). Rimmer has dealt with group marriage. His general point is that love is not exclusive and that the community that is formed by a number of loving people is much better than that formed by two. The latter tends toward possessiveness and alienation. The former, by eliminating possession while not affecting love, is an attack on alienation.

Heinlein's novel, one of the very few science fiction novels so far to express some of the ideas of the New Left, goes well beyond Rimmer to a complete bisexual sharing of love within a community. Here there is a complete expression of group sex as it relates to community. Sex is a major way of expressing feeling for others. Liberated sex means that people can freely have sexual relations with a number of loving partners. It is not the same as simple promiscuity, which usually has little if any sentiment involved. It means the free choice of partners based on sentiment. It is an expression of the closeness that community members feel for one another, the most complete expression of that closeness.

To many people, group sex may seem to be an extreme expression of the idea of community, but it should be seen as the natural outgrowth of the basic concept. Love is at the center of the new community; sex is an expression of love; therefore, sex becomes communal.

Loneliness, estrangement, isolation describe the vast distance between man and man today. These dominant tendencies cannot be overcome by better personnel management, nor by improved gadgets, but only when a love of man overcomes the idolatrous worship of things by man.[11]

Men and women must find and love other men and women both spiritually and physically. Only then will alienation be conquered. And this love is only possible within a community.

The New Left is highly community or communally oriented. This emphasis provides the basic social organization of the desired future society. If the family system, however much it is under fire and disintegrating, provides the basis of contemporary society, we can imagine that the family as we now know it—parents and children—will fade even more and be replaced with a tribe, clan, or commune. The new basis of society will not preclude the nuclear family as an entity, but considerably less emphasis will be placed on it.

The internal composition of the community could be fairly flexible, both within a given commune and across different communes. The wide range of possibilities might include, for example, racial or ethnic communes, those based on occupation, avocation, or area, or those based on sexual or familial characteristics. Many different combinations are possible—as many different combinations as there are different combinations of people.

Whatever the internal composition, the community will re-

---

11 "The Port Huron Statement," quoted in Paul Jacobs and Saul Landau, *The New Radicals: A Report with Documents* (New York: Vintage Books, 1966), p. 155.

place the family as the focus of loyalty for most people. This will happen because the family as we know it will no longer exist for large numbers of people and because the community or other structures within it will provide the love and security now derived from the family.

Again, communities will vary, but at least some of the following activities would be communal:

1. Child-rearing.
2. Cooking.
3. Domestic work—sewing, washing, etc.
4. Housekeeping, etc.
5. Other labor—farming, craft work or light industry.

In this way the new society will differ significantly from contemporary society. An individual will share most of his day-to-day activities with others to whom he is close. The work experience will not be rigidly separated from the other parts of life and the business of day-to-day work will be shared more equally than they are now. This will be particularly freeing for women.

The new communalism

The development of a community-based society is not the work of a moment, and the New Left is split over what to do now. One part tends to urban communes and either sees themselves as professional revolutionists or as activists of a less committed sort. The other part tends to live in rural communes and sees themselves either as creating the new society or are apolitical. Although there are many nuances to these positions, they represent the basic continuum of the New Left.

Many people either now live in communes, have lived in communes, plan to shortly, expect to some time, or wish they did. In addition, there are many communal pads or apartments where one can stay for a time while traveling. Therefore it can be fairly said that the New Left living arrangements are already becoming communal. There is a wave of communalism in the United States that is bigger than any of the past waves, which were quite large at times.

The tradition

In order to understand this new wave of communalism it will be instructive to look in some detail at previous communal movements, particularly those in the United States. This will demonstrate to what extent the current movement may actually be called "new."

A commune may be defined as an intentionally established community separated or withdrawn from contemporary society, the membership of which have shared values. It is probably impossible to say when the first commune was established, but we do know of the existence of Essene communities at the time of Christ. In the intervening years there have been hundreds if not thousands more.[12]

The contemporary movement has its major expression in the United States, and therefore will be stressed here. Moreover there is a reasonable amount of data available. One exception will be made—the Israeli Kibbutzim has had an important influence on the contemporary movement and will be discussed briefly.

The communitarians tend to be very enthusiastic about the advantages of communal living. One said that they "have collected factual proof that through the extraordinarily large economic advantage of common ownership of production and consumption of material goods, mankind will be safely, easily and quickly en-

---

[12] There is no good history of the communal movement in general. The interested reader will want to consult the following: Norman Cohn, *The Pursuit of the Millenium: Revolutionary Messianism in Medieval and Reformation Europe and Its Bearing on Modern Totalitarian Movements,* 2d ed. (New York: Harper and Row, 1961); E. V. Hobsbawm, *Primitive Rebels: Studies in Archaic Forms of Social Movement in the 19th and 20th Centuries* (New York: Frederick A. Praeger, 1959), and W. H. G. Armytage, *Heavens Below, Utopian Experiments in England 1560–1960* (London: Routledge and Kegan Paul, 1961).

riched."[13] Another, the founder of a rather short-lived religious commune of this century enumerated the advantages that he saw in this form of life as follows:

1. They had the great advantage of the collectivist organization in production.
2. They had equal distribution of goods.
3. They had none of the waste of competition.
4. They had none of the cost of distribution.
5. They had no unemployment and no strikes.
6. As all of the increment of wealth went to all the workers, there was the strongest motive for each to do his best work. No one could starve.
7. Where there was democracy there was a great advantage in the advice and counsel of the rank and file.
8. They had the peculiar asset of moral earnestness.
9. They had, presumably, no personal debts to worry about.
10. Their organization was conducive to sympathy, understanding and helpfulness.[14]

Obviously not everyone is as enthusiastic about communal living as these two communitarians, but it would be easy to provide many more similar such statements. Since the unverified statements of enthusiasts or detractors tell us little about the movement, however, let us look instead at a few of the communities.

The majority of communes in the United States, and all but one of those lasting over ten years, were religious, and therefore it is most appropriate to look first at these communities.[15]

---

[13] H. S. Albrecht, *Gegenwart und Zukunft; Unsere sozialen Zustände vor dem Richterstuhl der Gesunden Menschenvernunft, nebst Enteutungen, auf welche Weise ein vernünftig organisiertes Gesellschaftsleben erreichbar ist* (Philadelphia: F. W. Thomas und Söhne, [1873?]), pp. 9–10.

[14] Ralph Albertson, "A Survey of Mutualistic Communities in America," *Iowa Journal of History and Politics,* 34 (October 1936), p. 437. Reprinted by permission of the State Historical Society of Iowa.

[15] For lists of the communities, all of them incomplete, see Albertson, pp. 375–444; Arthur Bestor, *Backwoods Utopias: The Sectarian Origins and the Owenite Phase of Communitarian Socialism in America: 1663–1829,* 2d ed. (Philadelphia: University of Pennsylvania Press, 1970), pp.

The earliest experiments in the United States were of course in connection with the original settlements,[16] but the first withdrawn community seems to have been Plockhoy's Commonwealth,[17] a Dutch Mennonite Community, founded in 1663 in Delaware. It was destroyed a year later when the English conquered the area.

This community was followed by many small communities that withdrew from the society at large to practice their religion, which normally included the requirement of shared goods based on their reading of Christ's teaching. They withdrew in order to be free to follow their own sometimes unusual teachings.

Since it would be impossible to look at each community in any detail, I will attempt some generalizations about them with a few examples. Almost all the religious experiments had the following characteristics:

1. A charismatic leader.
2. An authoritarian political system.
3. Community property.

Some of the most successful also had unusual sexual systems, ranging from the celibacy practiced by the Shakers and others to the system of complex marriage (everyone married to everyone else) practiced by the Oneida Community. Most of the commu-

---

277–84, and Julia Elizabeth Williams, "An Analytical Tabulation of the North American Utopian Communities by Type, Longevity and Location," unpublished M.A. thesis, University of South Dakota, 1939.

[16] See Kenneth A. Lockridge, *A New England Town, The First Hundred Years: Dedham, Massachusetts, 1636–1736* (New York: W. W. Norton & Co., Inc., 1970). There were earlier experiments in South America, but they are beyond the scope of this book.

[17] A discussion of some of the ideas of the founder, Pieter Corneliszoon Plockhoy, can be found in J. K. Fuz, *Welfare Economics in English Utopias from Francis Bacon to Adam Smith* (The Hague: Martinus Nijhoff, 1952), pp. 55–62. The Community is discussed in Leland D. Harder, "Pioneer of Christian Civilization in America," *Mennonite Life,* 4 (January 1949), pp. 41–45; and Harder, "Plockhoy and his Settlement at Zwasnendael, 1663," *Delaware History,* 3 (March 1949), pp. 138–54.

nities, religious and secular, maintained the standard marriage and family systems.

Most of the religious communities were founded and led through their entire existence by a charismatic leader with a vision of a new religion within Christianity or the imminent coming of the millenium. Each community's religious practices were different, but they were all led by the vision of an unusual man or woman. Most did not survive the death of their founder. The few that did survive, such as the Shakers, were able to produce or attract very able men or women to lead them on an ongoing basis.

Most of the religious communities vested the positions of leadership with considerable authority. This was particularly true of the original leader, who was usually all-powerful, whatever formal limits were placed upon him. But it also seems to have held true for the succeeding leaders of the few communities that lasted beyond the death of their founders, though this generalization is open to dispute since studies of these communities have rarely dealt adequately with their internal political systems. This is not particularly surprising, since religion, not politics, was the central concern of the communities and they therefore de-emphasized the political, religious sanction often being more powerful than political.

All the religious communities practiced some form of community property. In most cases, property was owned by the community, and it provided the members with whatever they needed. Some of the religious communities were very successful economically and were able to provide very well for their members, although—even so—most led a fairly austere life. The majority of the communities were able to provide adequately for their members.

One problem plagued the long-lived communities: How to recruit for the celibate communities, or to retain their children for the others. The first problem was never completely solved by any of the celibate communities. (The Shakers, established in this country in 1776 and with a few members still remaining, came the closest.) The latter problem was much more serious for the secular communities, since the religious communities had the strength of their way of life plus the sanction of religion to hold their children, and they have held them fairly well.[18]

It is unclear what was the first secular community in the United States, but it was probably founded near the end of the 18th century or at the beginning of the 19th. The first major secular community was New Harmony, Indiana, founded by Robert Owen in 1825. Many Owenite communities followed New Harmony, but none lasted more than a few years.[19] Of the many secular communities that followed the New Harmony experiment, only a handful lasted more than a few years.

It is more difficult to generalize about the secular communities than about the religious ones. There was more divergence among the former, and the evidence about most of them is scant. About the only generalization that is safe is that almost all of them practiced some form of community property. Most seem to have followed the general practice of the religious communities, with the community holding all property and the members sharing on the basis of need. Others shared on the basis of labor and/or capital contributed, while a few had private property, with some communal facilities. None were particularly unsuccessful economically, but only a few were very successful.

Most never really got started and broke up after a few years. The few that lasted for many years were torn by internal dissension. Usually founded by a leader of some charisma, they had political systems ranging from the dictatorial to the anarchistic. Most seemed to have encouraged fairly extensive political participation by the members.

There is no real evidence that any secular communities had unusual marriage or family systems, although some did practice community child rearing. Generally, they were like most small

---

[18] See, for example, Victor Peters, *All Things Common: The Hutterian Way of Life* (Minneapolis: The University of Minnesota Press, 1965).

[19] See Bestor, passim.

farming communities, except for the practice of community property and, in some cases, the rejection of religion. Most did not last long enough to have a second-generation problem, but the ones that did, such as the series of seven Icarian communities, were fairly successful in keeping their children.[20] They were, though, constantly split by internal problems, one of which in Icaria was largely generational. The community split in two: the young group lasted thirteen years in two communities; the old group lasted twenty years in one community.

Thus the secular communities were less innovative and less successful than the religious communities, but both contributed significantly to what can only be called a tradition of communalism in this country. Over the years prior to this century, thousands of Americans participated in this movement by joining one of the many communes. Many more gave money to support one or more of the communes.

The phenomenon of communalism is not new in this country. It has been part of our history from the very beginning. It is an important part of our heritage. Although there was a period at the end of the 19th century and the beginning of the 20th in which few new communes were founded, the movement never stopped completely.

The Kibbutzim

Since the 1940s, the communal movement has been redeveloped in the American imagination by the Kibbutzim in Israel.[21] The Kibbutz movement has served the New Left as a symbol of the possibility of a successful collective economy within a larger society. Although the special conditions of the Kibbutzim have not been taken into account by the New Left, it believes that they have demonstrated the possibility of a successful communal movement within modern society. In 1967 there were 225 Kibbutzim

---

[20] See, for example, Marie Marchand Ross, *Child of Icaria* (New York: City Publishing Co., 1938).

[21] See the bibliography at the end of this book for some of the studies of the Kibbutzim.

with 93,210 members.[22] Although this represents only 3.93 percent[23] of the Jewish population of Israel, it is certainly sizable enough to be significant. A 4 percent minority in any country would be important.

In addition to its symbolic importance as a seemingly successful communal movement, the Kibbutz has also shown the practicability of communal child-rearing. Most of the Kibbutz have practiced some form of communal child-rearing, and in most cases the child stays in a communal children's house and the parents visit the child for a few hours each day. It seems to be generally believed that this is one of the most positive features of Kibbutz life,[24] and it is one of the features that is most applauded by the New Left. It is felt, for example, that this particular aspect of communal life is easily transferable to the society at large, and that day-care centers should be established in as many places as possible so that women may be free to spend their time as they choose and children can be exposed to wider horizons.

The communal movements in the United States and Israel have provided a tradition and a symbol for the new communal movement. It is too soon to be sure of its success or failure, and it has been too little studied, but it is of importance in understanding the New Left.

The new communal movement

It is impossible at this point in history to do much more than specify the major characteristics of the various types of communes that now exist and comment on some of the reasons for their successes and failures. Since many of them are planned as temporary

---

[22] Dan Leon, *The Kibbutz: A New Way of Life* (Oxford: Pergamon Press, 1969), p. 200.

[23] Ibid., p. 201.

[24] Many studies of communal child-rearing in Israel have been published in the past few years. See, for example, Peter B. Neubauer (ed.), *Children in Collectives: Child-Rearing Aims and Practices in the Kibbutz* (Springfield, Ill.: Charles C. Thomas, Publisher, 1965); and Melford E. Spiro, *Children of the Kibbutz* (Cambridge, Mass.: Harvard University Press, 1958).

experiments, the ending of a commune does not necessarily mean failure.

The existence of communes that are intended to be temporary is one of the greatest differences between the new movement and traditional communitarianism. The earlier communes, however temporary they may have been in actuality, were rarely, if ever, planned that way. Given vastly greater geographic mobility, an emphasis on the search for the self, and a recognition of change and impermanence, many of the new communes are created with the assumption that they will last a fairly short time.

This does not change the significance of the communal life style. Even if it appears that the commune is little different than the earlier pattern of individuals having temporary roommates, there are important differences. First, the groups are often mixed sexually. Second, and most important, the people in these groups think of themselves as living in communes. The attitude that we are now living a different life style that is better may be significant for the future. Even though the communes may be temporary, the people in them are likely to join other communes and be interested in experimenting with different living arrangements in the future.

The major divisions among communes today are urban-rural, religious-secular, permanent-temporary, activist-dropout. The typical urban commune is secular, temporary, and activist; the typical rural commune is secular, temporary, and dropout. There are, though, enough religious and supposedly permanent communes to include them as separate categories, but they compose a small minority of the total number of communes.

It is possible to make a number of generalizations about the current communities, and although it is possible to find exceptions to each of these generalizations, they seem valid. The major counter patterns are noted by way of contrast.[25]

The most universally correct generalization about the contem-

---

[25] These generalizations are based on many different sources. See the bibliography for the various sources.

porary communal movement is that the communes operate on the basis of community property. In other words, they share whatever property the community holds as a community along with whatever income is produced either by the community or by individual members of the community. Almost all of the contemporary communities operate on this basis, although there are some variations in the specifics.

Community property is, also, interestingly enough, one of the major causes of conflict within the contemporary commune. There are many examples in which an individual who has a significantly larger income than others in the community has felt as if he or she were supporting the community and has withdrawn from it. In addition, there have been serious problems in connection with the sharing of work within the commune. There is, first, the problem of some individuals not working; this is particularly a problem on some of the rural agricultural communes. Second, there is the problem of the division of labor between men and women in the communities, and this has caused considerable hard feelings on the part of the women.[26]

There are a few exceptions to the general rule of community property among the communes. The exceptions are primarily found in communities that started sometime in the post-World War II period and have managed to continue. There were not many of these, and few have lasted to the present. They did, though, provide two significant differences from the contemporary movement. First, their economic arrangements: the major capital goods of the community—land and expensive equipment—were owned communally and everything else was owned privately. Second, many were founded outside of North America, particularly in Australia and New Zealand. Today most communes are being established in the United States or Canada.

The general practice in the communities is to be governed by a process of participatory democracy.[27] Within the context of the

---

[26] See, for example, Vivian Estellachild, "Hippie Communes," *Women: A Journal of Liberation*, Vol. 2 (Winter 1971), pp. 40–43.

communities, this means that almost all decisions are made on the basis of consensus or by all those whom the question affects directly. In a commune, this is usually everyone. The communities meet regularly, once a week or more often, to discuss the basic problems of the community and to make decisions about them. The meetings are usually fairly free-wheeling and open.

Many of the communities find problems with the natural, day-to-day operation of this system. In particular they find difficulties with the enforcement of decisions that have been made by the community, since it is generally assumed that such decisions should be self-enforcing. Therefore, particularly with such supposedly self-enforcing decisions as work schedules and the like, communes have found some difficulty in getting the decisions followed.

There are a few exceptions to the general rule that communes operate on the basis of participatory democracy. Most of these exceptions are found in the religious communities in which there is a charismatic leader who has brought a number of disciples together around him. In these cases the leader makes most of the decisions, although often consulting with the membership of the commune, and the enforcement is primarily through the religious sanction.

One of the most respected ideals or goals of the communes is equality. In theory it is assumed that everyone within the commune is completely equal to everyone else in the commune and will be treated the same.[28] In practice there seems to be a problem in many of the communes with this concept. This is generally noted in the case of women, who are treated both as sexual objects by the men and as the appropriate people to do all of the domestic work. There are many reports of communes in which women are clearly treated as inferior by the men.

Another concept which is highly regarded within the com-

---

[27] See Chapter 6 for an extended discussion of the role this concept plays in the New Left.

[28] See Chapter 5 for an extended discussion of the role this concept plays in the New Left.

munal system is individual freedom. It is generally accepted that each individual within the community should not be interfered with by others within the community. Each individual should have as much freedom as possible to decide in what ways and to what extent he or she will participate in the day-to-day activities of the community or to what extent he or she will accept the rules and regulations of the community.

The problems with this concept generally seem to focus on the difficulty of getting the work done in the agricultural communes, and the relative lack of freedom that women possess in relationship to men in many of the communes. But in many cases it is believed that freedom is more important than getting the work done. Many of the members, having left home and school fairly recently, are understandably hesitant about any infringement of their freedom. The communal life is the great break with the unfreedom of the past and as such must be as free as possible. Fortunately for the survival of the communes, most people come to realize the need for self-imposed, cooperative limits on freedom, but much acrimonious dispute and many commune failures have resulted from this problem.

There are some communes in which the ideal of individual freedom has been severely limited because of these problems. In some communes work schedules have been established by the community. The option of the individual is either to adhere to the work schedule or leave the community. In this way some of the communities are attempting to overcome the problem of the individual who does not want to work. And in some of the religious communities the individual members also have their freedom somewhat limited by a series of daily activities which are part of their religious observances. This is, of course, a freely accepted limitation on freedom.

A practice that is almost universally accepted by the communities is communal child-rearing. Child-rearing by the nuclear family is considered bad, and it is generally argued that both for the good of the community and for the good of the parents and the children child-rearing should be communal. In the first place, many women would be removed from the labor force through spending time with children individually. In the second place, the women thus removed from the labor force are not free to develop their own interests because they are tied to their children. Thirdly, it is accepted that it is better for the children to be raised communally with contacts with a variety of children and adults than to be raised by individual families. This seems to be very widely accepted by the New Left as a whole, and though there are exceptions to the practice, they are rare.

Sexual relations within the communities are varied, and it is impossible to generalize about them. Sexual relations tend to be either wholly monogamous or mixed monogamous and group or communal sex. There are, in addition, communes which practice just communal or group sex. In addition to these, there are a number of communities that are gay but these follow the patterns already suggested—monogamous, communal, or mixed. Finally, there are a number of communes composed entirely of women that are *not* gay communes.

The communal movement represents the major attempt to practice the ideals of the New Left. It also often represents a split in the New Left. The dropouts are activists of a type that the revolutionists find hard to accept.[29] The revolutionists accept the communal approach and live in communes but still question or reject a major part of the communal movement.[30]

The idea of community is the central concept in New Left thought, but it is intimately connected with all the other concepts that make up the goals of the New Left. Probably the concept that is most closely linked to community is equality. Therefore, let us now turn to this idea—the one around which the whole movement had its beginning.

---

[29] For example, in *We Are Everywhere* (New York: Harper & Row, 1971), p. 157, Jerry Rubin argues against the dropout.

[30] See Chapter 7 for a discussion of the controversy surrounding tactical questions.

5

EQUALITY

The concept of equality gives the most interesting illustration of the development of New Left thought from an initial acceptance of reform within the system, to a questioning of the possibility for such reform, and, finally, for some at least, to the advocacy of revolution. In this chapter I shall first look at the concept of equality to see what it means and what it has meant. Then I shall look at the New Left critique of equality in contemporary society. Next I shall look at the way equality has been used in New Left thought. Finally, two movements particularly important to the development of contemporary American radical thought, black radicalism and the women's liberation movement, will be discussed. It should be obvious that these movements were chosen because they represent the most complete questioning of the meaning of equality in contemporary radical thought. It would have been possible to look at other aspects of New Left activity, such as that among the poor, but the black and women's movements raise many more questions about equality than does the movement with the poor. Also, since most of the work in poverty has taken place among the blacks rather than among the poor whites, except in Appalachia, it is possible to build into a discussion of black radicalism some considerations of the movement among the poor.

In order to fully understand what the rather vague term *equality* means, it is important to look at some of its possible meanings

57

and some of the ways in which it is being used. In mathematics, the equals sign ($=$) means that one side of an equation is the exact equivalent of the other side of the equation, but in social and political thought, the term equality refers to something much more complicated. To put it another way, in mathematics if one side of the equation does not exactly balance the other side of the equation, there is no equality. In social and political life, there will never be a situation in which there is that sort of perfect equality; the equation will never exactly balance without some sort of breeding system such as that found in Aldous Huxley's *Brave New World* (1932).

At the simplest level, political equality comes about as close to the mathematical notion of equality as it is possible to come in social and political life. This is particularly true at the most simple level of the problem, the vote. In voting, equality means that each citizen has one vote. It also means that each vote will be counted in exactly the same way and be given exactly the same weight as every other vote in determining the result.

Unfortunately, political life is not as simple as this sounds. First, there is the problem of the definition of citizen. At one level we have the disenfranchisement of all those under some specified age, and there are a variety of other exclusions that limit the number of citizens eligible to vote. And then there is money. Even though the rich man has his vote counted the same as the poor man, the rich man has considerably more opportunities to affect the choice of candidates who will run in elections, and, by donating money to the candidate of his choice, he has considerably more power in determining the outcome, or at least in helping to determine the outcome, of an election.

Another invidious factor can be seen in the controversy over reapportionment. In a large and populous country it seems necessary to have a representative system of government,[1] and in estab-

---

[1] Most members of the radical part of the New Left reject this contention. Others question the general notion but have not rejected it, and some accept it.

lishing a representative system of government, the country is divided into a number of voting districts, each one of which elects a representative. For example, if country or state X has a population of 100,000,000 which is divided into ten electoral districts it is fairly obvious that each electoral district should have 10,000,000 people in it. In that way each of the 10,000,000 people (here we have the problem of the complicating factor of citizenship) could be expected to have exactly the same weight in determining the outcome of the election. If, on the other hand, the districts vary in size from, for example, 250,000 people to 20,000,000 people, we can see that the individual in the district with only 250,000 people has the possibility of having considerably greater impact on the election than does the person in the district with 20,000,000 people. Therefore, unless the districts contain exactly, or as nearly as exactly as possible, the same number of people, there is no political equality.

Legal equality is another area in which it is fairly simple to define what we mean by equality, but in which there are complicating factors that produce a situation in which equality does not exist. Legal equality means that each individual will be treated exactly the same by the legal system. By extension, this means that each individual will be treated the same by the courts, the police, and all other agencies of the law. Such equality is of course affected by such factors as money and race.

A third aspect of equality is economic equality. Here again it is possible to conceive of economic equality in purely mathematical terms. It could be defined, as Edward Bellamy did in *Looking Backward 2000–1888* (1888), so that it would mean each individual receives exactly the same dollar amount or its equivalent in income each year. Now, this certainly does define a form of economic equality and in a wealthy society—that is, one in which there is no scarcity—it would undoubtedly be the best. But we live in a world of scarcity. Therefore most would argue either for bringing together the extremes or for a distribution of economic power (income or other control of resources) which would make it possible for each person to realize his potentials. (The latter is more truly economic equality than simply bringing together the extremes, but the former has been considered part of such equality and so I include it here.)

The basic assumption of both of these approaches is that people need an improved, equal or more nearly equal, chance to fulfill themselves. The traditional myth of capitalism is that any two individuals, no matter what their differences at the beginning, can achieve success. Success is, unfortunately, an ambiguous concept, but in the myth, at least, success seems to be most often equated with making great amounts of money. A perusal of the Horatio Alger stories that so popularized this myth points out some rather interesting facts. In these stories the hero invariably starts out as a poor, starving, but worthy boy. He manages to become an office boy or something of the sort in a successful firm or in one that has the potential for success. Through dint of hard work, ability, and *incredible good luck* the poor no longer, starving no longer, but still worthy young man becomes owner of the company and marries his ex-boss's daughter, who is rich but worthy. The key to his success of course is found in the phrase "incredible good luck"—that is, hard work and ability alone will not win out.

One example should suffice. In a number of Alger stories success comes to the worthy hero through rescuing the boss's daughter from a runaway team of horses. Now the number of times that your boss's daughter may be imperiled by a runaway team of horses—with you on the appropriate corner to rescue her—is miniscule. If you spend all of your time standing around on possible appropriate corners, either you will be fired for wasting your time, or the boss's daughter will not ever be imperiled by a run-away team of horses. There are of course other alternatives—the team runs away with the boss's daughter on another corner, or you completely bungle the job of rescuing the boss's daughter, or the boss's daughter is already married and rescuing her won't do you much good anyway because the son-in-law is going to inherit the company, or the boss has a son who is going to inherit the company.

Of course what equality of opportunity should mean is that our poor, starving, but worthy young man (or woman) should be able to achieve success without incredible good luck. If equality of opportunity is taken to mean that two individuals of exactly the same ability can achieve the exact same success economically without significantly different effort or luck while one of them is poor and starving and the other is the son of a millionaire, clearly the concept is ridiculous.

The final and most complex part of equality, social equality, is so nebulous a concept that discussing it may be of little use in bringing about an understanding of equality. But it is precisely in these vague and nebulous areas that it is necessary to attempt to clarify the concept. Social equality, although difficult to define, is still an important notion. It is possible to begin to grasp some of its import by thinking of the somewhat more rigid class system that used to exist in this country. While laws prohibiting social inter-course rarely existed, it was impossible for individuals of different social classes to communicate with each other. This separation was accomplished by a variety of subtle and obvious distinctions. In the first place, certain areas were either legally or effectively out of bounds for certain classes. This would include upper-class clubs, certain areas at the race tracks or certain races; certain sports considered to be available only to the upper classes; and certain areas of town reserved for one class or the other. By rarely if ever seeing one another, communication was limited if not eliminated. While some of the more obvious of these restrictions have been done away with, a little thought will persuade anyone that many of the barriers still exist. For example, the pattern of housing rarely brings people with very different social backgrounds into contact.

Looking at sexual equality as one aspect of social equality, it is easy to see ways in which women are treated unequally. In the first and most obvious case, women are often treated as merely an appendage of a man. One fairly simple example would be the typical bar or tavern in which a woman who is not with a man is often considered "fair game" for the men in the bar. It is not enough to say that some women encourage such attention; it is the expectations that are accepted in the situation rather than the individual preferences involved.

The New Left is not of one mind on many things and the approach to equality is one of those many things. The positions it takes range from reform now to revolution now. The reformer often would like to see revolution as the solution to the problem, but feels that it may be too long in coming and that in the meantime reform is essential.

This is the classical problem of every revolutionist. The rejection of reform may lose support because it seems to reject the immediate amelioration of bad conditions. But if the revolutionist accepts reform and the reform works, the revolution is bound to be delayed.[2]

The New Left is caught in this dilemma and it is reflected most particularly in its approach to equality (due, in large part, to the history of the movement). Therefore, in the analysis that follows I shall look at both the reformist approach and the long-range goals, but it must be remembered that the reformist also accepts the goals.

The New Left critique

If the beginning of the American New Left is dated with the development of the civil rights movement, which seems to be a fairly accurate statement, the first demand was equality in the South. It was a request for reform within the system—and a rather peculiar type of reform at that: a reform that merely asked for the enforcement on an equal basis of the laws of the country. In other words, the original request was for a reform that was easily defensible within the country's legal and political structure as it then existed. This did not mean that getting the reform was any easier than it would have been if it had constituted a challenge to the law, but at the beginning the request for equality was simply a request for reform.

---

[2] The classic revolutionist response is found in Lenin's *"Left-Wing" Communism, An Infantile Disorder*. There are many editions available.

The history of the civil rights movement in the United States has been told many times, and it would not be of particular value to retell it again here. If anyone wonders why the civil rights movement moved gradually from request to demand, from a southern-based movement to a nationwide movement with focus on the South, from gradual minimal reform to immediate reform or revolution, he need merely reread that history.[3]

The civil rights movement did move from reform to a much more radical stance. Many northern white and black students were involved in the civil rights movement in the South, and it should come as no surprise that the one group had an effect on the other so that the next major stage of the shift from reform to revolution was seen in the development of a northern student movement. On many college campuses a small percentage of the apathetic generation of the '50s had been becoming less apathetic and begun requesting the reforms. These requests were rejected and since the students did not have the power to put pressure on the system, nothing was accomplished.

In one case, that of the University of California at Berkeley, this movement has been traced out over a number of years by a number of writers.[4] Here again there was a long period of request for reform before the explosion. Here again was the pattern of movement from reform being requested to reform being demanded, a pattern of movement from reform to revolution, a matter of a fairly powerless group requesting reform and being denied it, with the later addition of large numbers of people because a variety of incidents gave power to the powerless whose requests were still being denied. It would be foolish to expect a powerless group that gained power to remain as silent as it had before it gained power. The denial of reform to a powerful group will move that group in the direction of revolution.

In each case of protest throughout the country, a group developed an identity and some power. In each case the realization

---

[3] A few works are suggested in the bibliography.
[4] A few works are suggested in the bibliography.

that there were many with similar problems led to a solidarity within the group that helped to escalate the demands of the group. This escalation was reflected in the criticism that was made of contemporary society. This criticism consisted of a blast at virtually all contemporary institutions as being infected with the disease of prejudice and its resultant inequality. Of course the black was the most obvious case, but the Chicano, the American Indian, the longhaired or bearded, women, the gay, and many others found that they were targets of overt and covert hostility and hatred.

The emphasis was first put on racism. ". . . racism is a natural product of the history, culture, and socio-politico-economic structure of the United States."[5] Because women came to recognize that they were as exploited as the blacks, adding sexism to racism in the above quotation would make it more correct.[6]

Here is the first focus of concern in the New Left attack on inequality in American society: the assertion, argument, and evidence of prejudice, racism, and sexism. The evidence came with the attack on civil rights workers in the North and the South and with the growing recognition by women, and even men,[7] that women were repressed—and of course there are the various other minority movements that have started in the past few years. But while the identification of prejudice, racism, and sexism is important, the identification of the causes is more important.

The central focus in the search for causes has been the political and economic systems of the United States. And this search has led to an even broader commentary on inequality in American society. The New Left sees political inequality stemming from the lack of participation in the political system by the vast majority

---

[5] Frank Joyce, "Racism in the United States: An Introduction," in Long (ed.), op. cit., p. 129.

[6] The literature on the suppression of women is growing rapidly. For a basic summary see the section entitled "The Oppressed Majority: The Way It Is," in Robin Morgan (ed.), op. cit., pp. 31–157.

[7] Jerry Rubin admits in *We Are Everywhere* that he had not recognized his own sexism until recently. See for example, pp. 208–9.

of people, a lack of participation which, according to the New Left, is encouraged by the political system. In the first place, political questions are presented as being too complex for the average person. Secondly, the political system is seen as being dominated by an elite which is not responsive to the needs and wishes of the people. Politics is viewed as a competition between individuals who project images that have been manufactured by public relations firms to appeal to the greatest number of possible voters. The voter is simply presented with two candidates who are not significantly different.[8] Thus the voter either falls back on some tradition of voting for a particular party, or he fails to vote.

The New Left sees the American voter as deluded, repressed, and without real choice. The New Left believes that the issues presented to the voter are unreal and manufactured for the specific purpose of obtaining votes. It believes that the real issues are suppressed, and that the voter is tricked into believing that there are no other issues. The myth of majority rule and democracy is maintained by periodical elections which, however, give the voter a choice between two candidates who do not significantly disagree, who both have been manufactured by public relations men, and who are dependent upon men with money to get themselves elected.[9]

Thus, political equality depends ultimately on the economic system. The rich can contribute to political campaigns and can thus insure that their point of view is represented or at least listened to, but the average citizen has no such opportunity. He is too busy earning his living (in an uninteresting occupation) to

---

[8] A number of years ago a novel presented a presidential election in which both candidates rigidly followed their PR advisors' advice and ended up doing the same things. See John G. Schneider, *The Golden Kazoo* (New York: Rinehart, 1956).

[9] See Carl Oglesby, "Trapped in a System" (sometimes entitled "Let Us Shape the Future"), in Massimo Teodori (ed.), *The New Left: A Documentary History* (Indianapolis, Ind.: The Bobbs-Merrill Co., 1969), pp. 182–88. Although this article discusses corporate liberalism in general, its relevance for a discussion of political inequality is clear.

spend any significant part of his time involved in politics. He has been trained to believe that the possession of material goods is the highest goal that he can achieve and he spends his money on them, his time on acquiring the money. He has been duped, of course, since more and more possessions will only enslave him even further.[10]

The New Left thus is not merely critizing the existence of economic inequality, then, although they focus on that inequality. They are most concerned with consumerism or the constant piling up of more and more unnecessary material possessions that tie people to unrewarding jobs so that they can earn the money to pay for them.

The New Left believes that an attack on consumerism is a fundamental attack on the capitalist system, since capitalism could not exist without the "need" for unnecessary goods. Also, the New Left notes the "planned obsolesence" that is part of the manufacturing process so that individuals will "re-need" the same item within a relatively short period of time, thus keeping business busy producing replacements for its own products.[11]

This attack on the capitalist system is also an attack on economic inequality since it points out that no one except the rich man is free to choose his own life style. Only the rich are capable of escaping the nine to five drudgery of the working man. Only the rich are capable of obtaining the positions that allow them the truly good things of life. The individual with an average income is tricked into believing that the things he can buy are in fact the good things in life, but, according to the New Left, he really knows that they are not, and he is thus deeply alienated from the system. (At the same time he cannot admit that he has been fooled and attacks all those who attempt to show him his error.)

Equality of opportunity, according to the New Left, is simply

---

[10] See Dave Gilbert, "Consumption: Domestic Imperialism," in Long (ed.), op. cit., pp. 26–42.

[11] See the section entitled, "Culture and Advanced Capitalism," in Lothstein (ed.), op. cit., pp. 133–270.

a delusion that has been created by the capitalist system to trick the dissident into attempting to achieve a higher income and the ability to buy a car and a color TV set.[12] The New Left argues that even if equality of opportunity were possible, it would be a delusion because what is achieved is not worth achieving. And since equality of opportunity only means an average income, is it worth the bother? And since the system needs some poor at the bottom to take the seasonal jobs and the like—"an acceptable un-employment rate"—there cannot be any equality of opportunity. Since nothing is done to make it meaningful, it is simply another delusion fostered to keep the population content. Unless the culture of poverty is overcome, unless the educational system within the central cities is made meaningfully equivalent to the educational system in the suburbs and in the private schools, equality of opportunity is meaningless. The individual coming out of the ghetto who does not have models of success within the system will not try. The individual coming out of the ghetto who is trained in the schools of the central city will never have a chance. Thus, equality of opportunity cannot exist without radical changes within the system.

The New Left also argues that there can be no equality before the law because the legal system is simply a reflection of the wishes of the elite. They point to the trial of the Chicago Seven, in which the judge appeared to be clearly biased against the de-fendants, as an example.[13] They argue that the courts demand that the accused fit into the style of the middle-class white or be presumed guilty until he proves himself innocent. Any challenge to the court system is treated harshly. Also, the New Left argues that the police, as representatives of the powerful, do not even

---

[12] John H. Schaar argues that the concept is philosophically weak in "Equality of Opportunity and Beyond," in J. Roland Pennock and John W. Chapman (eds.), *Nomos IX, Equality: Yearbook of the American Society for Political and Legal Philosophy* (New York: Atherton Press, 1967), pp. 228–249.

[13] See Tom Hayden, *Trial* (New York: Holt, Rinehart & Winston, 1970), and Jerry Rubin, *We Are Everywhere*.

pretend to treat the dissident and the poor as they treat the middle class and the rich.

The cop is a phenomenon, unto himself. He is a paranoid. He is a megalomaniac. He can be a sadist. He can be viscious and cruel. He can be nice and sweet, especially if he wants something. He can break the laws that he pretends to be enforcing, with impunity. He is very sensitive to being called names, and tends to react the only way he knows how. He is armed to the teeth, with clubs, chemicals, gases, firearms, and the most frightening weapon of all, righteous indignation. He tends to be stupid, and uneducated, and very aware of his shortcomings. . . .[14]

Finally, there is social inequality. This is both a cause of and a reflection of the other inequalities. In some areas we are just becoming aware of the way we treat many individuals. We are just becoming aware of sexist humor as we only recently became aware of racist humor. We have only begun to realize the ways in which and the extent to which we degrade women in everyday life, as we only became aware a few years ago of the images of the black man that were projected on television and in the other media. We have just begun to notice the similar images that we project about the American Indian, the Chicano, and the Oriental. We had assumed that any difference from the white, middle-class, Anglo-Saxon Protestant was bad. Equality we have defined as becoming like a white, middle-class, Anglo-Saxon Protestant. This is perhaps the most devastating and cruel concept of equality that is possible. We have assumed that only one life style is good, that only one sex is good, that only one religion is good, that only one national background is good. We have written into our laws that this is not true, but we have assumed in our lives that it is. Our humor, our images of others, and our treatment of others has shown up the falsehood of our laws, but we have only recently begun to notice it.

Social equality is the most subtle and the most difficult of the

---

[14] William Powell, *The Anarchist Cookbook* (New York: Lyle Stewart, Inc., 1971), p. 154.

concepts of equality, but it is probably the most important. If the New Left movement has done nothing else, it has brought to the attention of both the minorities and the majorities the ways in which we subtly oppress.

The New Left position on equality

Contemporary radical thought approaches equality from two different angles. The first approach is to maintain the reformist stance of the past. In other words, it attempts to deal with the question of equality within the system. The second approach rejects the system as it exists today and wishes to replace it with a system which is essentially different. The reformist approach does not reject the idea of revolution; revolution is accepted, but reform is considered necessary now since revolution may not occur for some time.[15]

I shall look briefly at the reformist approach first and then turn to the revolutionary approach. The reformist approach focuses today on a relatively limited number of questions, which may be summarized as follows:

1. Greater political power to the poor and the minorities.
2. Real equality before the law.
3. Reduction of the level of poverty.
4. Specific reforms in the status of women—for example, equal pay for equal work.

The first two of these reforms depend on a series of reforms that would give more power to determine their own lives directly to the people. The specific reform that is envisioned under point one is that political power be reallocated on a community basis. In other words, everyone should be consulted with regard to any programs or decisions that affect them directly. Thus, for example, the poor should be much more intimately involved in the day-to-day operation of the welfare system. They should be consulted

---

[15] See Chapter 7 for a further discussion of this problem.

on any changes, such as urban renewal, that are to be made in the areas they live. This consultation might take a number of forms, but the emphasis is on direct involvement, particularly on the part of the poor and the minorities. The point entails a basic criticism of the system of representation that we have today. Since the poor are weak politically, the politicians have ignored them. Now the poor are demanding recognition and greater involvement in the political process.

Reform in equality before the law focuses on two groups—the police and the lawyers. It is a truism that the poor and the minorities are treated differently by the police than are the upper-middle-class white. Since police are the representatives of the government and the legal system that people meet most often and most directly, and since the police often and obviously discriminate against the poor and the minorities, an intolerable situation is created. The police and the community in which they work must come to understand each other better and overcome the prejudice that has been built up over years of hostility.

The role of the lawyer in achieving equality for the poor and the minorities is particularly important. The poverty lawyer and the civil liberties lawyer are the greatest hopes that the poor and the minorities have of being given an equal or fair hearing in the court room. The court system, by demanding sets of behavior and attitudes that are not common to the poor and the minorities, discriminates greatly against them. The court system is designed for the white middle-class, who seldom use it, though when they do they can afford expensive lawyers.

Attempts to modify the welfare system with a view to reducing poverty have not been of prime importance in reformist thought. The most important reform economically has been in the attempt, noted in point four above, to achieve equality for women.

But most of the reformist elements in New Left thought have disappeared. The New Left today is more reformist on the question of equality than on any other question, because it is still concerned with achieving a greater degree of equality for the poor, the minorities, and women, but it is shifting to the position that reform is not the correct approach for achieving this end. The New Left has moved and is still moving toward more radical solutions for the problems of equality. What follows is more typical of the focus of the New Left. The New Left sees the solutions to the problems of inequality in contemporary society to be:

1. Participatory democracy in politics and law.[16]
2. Economic equality through democratic socialism.
3. Radical social equality.

Economic equality through democratic socialism is an ever more important goal of the New Left. The New Left is beginning to argue that the capitalist system is incapable of changing itself sufficiently to meet the needs of a new society. Only socialism, democratically controlled, is capable of recognizing and meeting our needs. We must achieve greater economic equality in order to free individuals from the drudgery of boring jobs and consumerism. If a man has a decent income, he can be freer with his own life style. If he is able to live as he wishes, he will be more creative and more productive of things that are of value to society.

The use of the vague phrase "democratic socialism" to describe the route the New Left wants to take economically is intended. The New Left has not contributed significantly to economic discussion. In its criticism of capitalism, it has simply taken over the basis of the Marxian analysis with a few additions regarding the affects of consumerism.[17] On its positive side, the New Left talks about socialism and workers' control.[18]

It is, though, possible to construct the basic characteristics of the future economy as seen by the New Left:

---

[16] See Chapter 6 for a discussion of these points.

[17] See, for example, Paul A. Baran and Paul M. Sweezy, *Monopoly Capital; An Essay on the American Economic and Social Order* (New York: Monthly Review Press, 1966), Herbert Marcuse, *An Essay on Liberation* (Boston: Beacon Press, 1969), and David Horowitz, "The Fate of Midas: A Marxist Interpretation of the American Social Order," in Lothstein (ed.), op. cit., pp. 184–205.

[18] See Paul Mattick, "Workers' Control", in Long (ed.), pp. 376–98.

1. Production
   a) Agricultural communes produce for themselves and urban areas
   b) Agricultural areas develop light industries and crafts
   c) Urban areas aim at self-sufficiency in both agriculture and industry—which means gradual elimination of large cities
   d) Production controlled either by the workers in the industry or by the community
2. Distribution
   a) Primarily within the community
   b) Some essential trade
3. Consumption
   a) To each according to his need
   b) Elimination of unreal needs

This last point is one of the most important. The New Left wishes to achieve economic equality through a rejection of consumerism and materialism. Its members wish to move away from a society whose main goal is to pile up more and more goods to a society that is concerned with the individual and the community. By doing away with much of today's waste production and removing many unnecessary products from the market, man should, according to New Left theorists, be able to produce the necessities of life and the artistic luxuries through a shorter work day and a greater emphasis on the creative arts and crafts.

The experience of the movement is one of voluntary and involuntary poverty. Money is an important distinction between those in the movement and those who are greedy or have been bought. Radicals who earn more than a subsistance share material identity with the ambitious and have sold out. And because they do not share the state of poverty they are outside the psychological community that the mystique about poverty has created in the movement. Poverty is thus a de facto prerequisite to full status in the radical community.[19]

---

[19] Barbara and Alan Haber, "Getting By with a Little Help from Our Friends," in Long (ed.), p. 296.

Although the idea of poverty after the revolution is not involved, the mystique of poverty symbolizes the reduction of needs. If need can be significantly reduced, the economic system can work in the way the New Left visualizes. If need cannot be so reduced, the economic system cannot so work.

The reduction of unnecessary needs is of course directly related to the search for the self. Material goods get in the way of finding the real self. A person defines himself by his goods and misses anything deeper.

The new man will live in a commune in which he will, with the other members of the commune, work to produce the necessities of life and some few luxuries. He will not be burdened by his material possessions and he will, through this rejection of materialism, be able to come closer to a rediscovery of himself and his relationship to the world and his community. The attempt to achieve economic equality through socialism and anti-materialism is thus closely related to the basic concepts of community and self that I have noted earlier.

One of the most interesting aspects of New Left thought today is the growing emphasis on social equality. For the New Left, the old equality of trying to become as much like white, Anglo-Saxon Protestants as possible is dead. The new equality asserts that the differences among human beings are there, and they are good. It *is* different to be black, and it is good; it *is* different to be a Chicano, and it is good; it *is* different to be a woman, and it is good—all this being an assertion that there are different life styles and values connected with these differences. These life styles and these values have been hidden or almost lost in attempts to copy the white, Anglo-Saxon Protestant, but they have not been lost altogether, and they will, it is asserted, be developed again. Social equality means that all people will be treated in the same way— as individuals—by the political and legal systems, and that the important differences among people will not be lost.

The communal system will probably represent this aspect of equality. Communes can be established on the basis of these differences. Blacks may want to form communes only with other blacks; women may want to form communes only with other women; Chicanos may want to form communes only with other Chicanos. This could be true of other groups in society also. It is hoped that by the recognition and development of these differences within the human race it will be possible for the different communes to cooperate without prejudice and animosity. Each individual and each group should have the power to individually make the decision of how to live. No model (such as the white, Anglo-Saxon Protestant) should be forced upon any individual or group. The commune system and participatory democracy are devices for insuring that social equality can in fact thrive, that the differences among men can in fact be recognized and encouraged.

Black radicalism

Here I am concerned with the basic ideas of contemporary black radicalism. The picture is hard to construct and many of the details are unclear because the Movement itself is not completely agreed upon them—but fortunately the main outlines are clear. The development of black radicalism in the United States has been complex. The familiar reform posture gradually gave way to a more radical and revolutionary posture. Heros came and went. Groups were formed, grew or didn't, split, and some died.[20]

The central focus of black radicalism has been criticism of the American system—economically, politically, and socially. The system is attacked as racist to the core and incapable of reform.

---

[20] Some of the relevant documents can be found in Floyd B. Barbour (ed.), *The Black Power Revolt; A Collection of Essays* (Boston: Extending Horizons Books, 1968); Francis L. Broderick and August Meier (eds.), *Negro Protest Thought in the Twentieth Century* (Indianapolis, Ind.: The Bobbs-Merrill Co., Inc., 1965); Richard P. Young (ed.), *Roots of Rebellion; The Evolution of Black Politics and Protest Since World War II* (New York: Harper & Row, Publishers, 1970); and Herbert J. Storing (ed.), *What Country Have I? Political Writings by Black Americans* (New York: St. Martin's Press, 1970).

"We have come to comprehend the nature of racism. It is a mass psychosis."[21] The American system is compared to the colonial regimes that European countries ran in Africa and Asia,[22] and only rarely were these regimes changed without revolution. One analysis notes that all colonization, external (the colonization of the underdeveloped countries) and internal (the ghettos in the United States), has four characteristics.

1. "Colonization begins with a forced, involuntary entry"—the slave trade.
2. Destruction of ". . . indigenous values, orientations, and ways of life."
3. Control by outsiders—white control of blacks and black neighborhoods.
4. Racism.[23]

Since racism is seen to permeate the entire system, no real change is possible until the system is destroyed.[24] "Racism . . . can't be destroyed under the capitalist system."[25]

Still, since black radicals identify closely with the black ghetto dweller, they recognize the need to accept whatever reforms can

---

[21] Robert F. Williams, *Negroes with Guns* (New York: Marzani and Munsell, 1962), p. 110.

[22] Along this line, the works of Frantz Fanon are very popular among black radicals. See *The Wretched of the Earth,* trans. Constance Farrington (New York: Grove Press, 1965); *Toward the African Revolution (Political Essays),* trans. Haakon Chevalier (New York: Grove Press, 1967); and *Black Skins, White Masks,* trans. Charles Lam Markman (New York: Grove Press, 1967).

[23] Robert Blauner, "International Colonialism and Ghetto Revolt," in Edward Greer (ed.), *Black Liberation Politics; A Reader* (Boston, Mass.: Allyn and Bacon, Inc., 1971), p. 351.

[24] Some of the best critiques are found in two autobiographical works— Eldridge Cleaver, *Soul on Ice* (New York: Dell Publishing Co., 1968); and Malcolm X, *The Autobiography of Malcolm X* (New York: Grove Press, 1965).

[25] H. Rap Brown, *Die Nigger Die* (New York: Dial Press, 1969), p. 124.

be obtained on the road to revolution.[26] Daily they see the horrible living conditions of their brothers and sisters, and they cannot turn their backs or they may lose their right to speak. This attitude complicates the study of black radicalism. It appears reformist and revolutionary in turn, and it is, but the reform streak is growing less important.

In analyzing black radicalism, it is possible to focus on three concepts: (1) black consciousness, (2) black power, and (3) nationalism or separation. The first two are important elements in the thought of all black radicals. The third is less agreed upon, but it is still a central element in the thinking of many, and it is clearly of growing importance.

Stressing these three concepts does not mean that they exhaust the range of black radical thought, because they certainly do not, but they are the key concepts. The rest of black radical thought is not significantly different from the thought of the rest of the New Left. In fact, black consciousness reflects three of the themes already discussed in this book: the search for the authentic self, community, and social equality; black power and nationalism or separation reflect others. The terms used by the black radicals are different, but the ideas are not greatly so.[27] The most obvious difference is over the amount of government control permissible in the future society, particularly control of the economy. Blacks tend to favor more direct, central control than does the rest of the New Left.

Black consciousness

One of the most important slogans of the Movement is "Black Is Beautiful." In American culture black has been the symbol of

---

[26] One of the most brilliant pleas for reform is Stokely Carmichael's and Charles V. Hamilton's *Black Power: The Politics of Liberation in America* (New York: Vintage Books, 1967). The book calls for far-reaching change, but it is essentially reformist.

[27] The greatest split between the black movement and the "traditional" New Left is over tactics. This split will be discussed at the end of this section and more generally in Chapter 7.

evil and ugliness. The discovery that "Black Is Beautiful" was the most important step away from an acceptance of an inferior status. "The call for black consciousness is at first painfully hard to answer. It's hard to start all over again and establish new principles and modes of operation. For we have struggled vainly for so long, trying to approximate white culture!"[28] Here is the recognition of what I have called social equality. Blacks have been taught that they are inferior, but by the development of black consciousness they have moved a significant step away from that feeling.

Black consciousness then is a central element in black radical thought. It asserts, "I'm no ordinary human. I am different."[29] It rejects the standard of whiteness and asserts the value of blackness. For the black there could never be an authentic self as long as whiteness was the standard. The black was totally alienated, but with the recognition that "Black Is Beautiful," the road away from alienation was opened.

To be taught that skin color was a mark of inferiority degrades a black into trying to emulate the white either by "passing" or by getting a "conk" to straighten his hair. As long as whiteness remained the goal, the black suffered the worst kind of alienation— he hated himself, and his family and friends all reminded him of his blackness. He could not help but be alienated until he discovered that "Black Is Beautiful." The Afro and the dashiki are symbols of an emancipation as great as that from slavery. They symbolize the rejection of the white standard.

But the hate of self that was built up has now been transferred to "whitey" or the "honkey." Any white man who asks himself, "What do 'they' want?" or "why do 'they' hate me? I've always supported 'them'," simply cannot have thought about the problem. Eldridge Cleaver and Malcolm X portray beautifully the process by which a black man used to be, and still often is, de-

---

[28] Jean Smith, "I Learned to Feel Black," in Barbour (ed.), p. 218.
[29] John E. Johnson, Jr., "Super Black Man," in Barbour (ed.), p. 225.

stroyed by white society and the tremendous intelligence, guts, and luck that are needed to overcome it. And they show the hate that comes too.[30]

Black consciousness asserts community. "Think Black" focuses the attention of all blacks on themselves, their culture, and their history, all of which has been ignored by white culture and society. "The love we seek to encourage is within the black community, the only American community where men call each other 'brother' when they meet."[31] The creation of black consciousness makes this possible.

Black power

Whereas the phrase "Black consciousness "immediately gives rise to the intended image, the phrase "black power" does not. It is closely related to black consciousness—"Before a group can enter the open society, it must first close ranks."[32] The recognition of the positive nature of blackness is the first step in closing ranks.

Beyond that, black power relates closely to participatory democracy: blacks must have control of their own communities. Blacks must have the political and economic power in their communities; their communities must not be run by whites as they have been in the past. And black power means that blacks should have "an effective share in the total power of the society."[33]

The concept is not limited to politics and economics, but its central focus is there.[34] Its central focus is there because the ability to change is found most directly in politics and economics; they

---

[30] In addition to Cleaver, op. cit., and Malcolm X, op. cit., see William H. Grier and Price M. Cobbs, *Black Rage* (New York: Basic Books, 1968.)

[31] Stokely Carmichael, "Power and Racism," in Barbour (ed.), p. 70.

[32] Carmichael and Hamilton, p. 44.

[33] Ibid., p. 47.

[34] See National Black Economic Development Conference, "The Black Manifesto," in Sondra Silverman (ed.), *The Black Revolt and Democratic Politics* (Lexington, Mass.: D. C. Health and Co., 1970), pp. 75–79, for a broad statement of Black power. See also, Chuck Stone, "The National Conference on Black Power," in Barbour (ed.), pp. 189–98.

are the most apparent vehicles of power. And since black radicals are concerned with bringing power to the black community, they are primarily concerned with political and economic questions.

The specific suggestions involved are many and varied. Here we can list only a few:

1. Black business in black communities.
2. Black people represented by black officials.
3. Black education—both content and control.
4. Black control of agencies operating in black communities.
5. Black banks.
6. Black credit unions.
7. Black police in black communities.
8. Black police boards in black communities.
9. Black apprentice programs in unions.
10. Black publishing companies.

These points are not inclusive, and they do not illustrate the entire range of concerns of black radicals, but they are suggestions of that range. They are also suggestions of the appeal that nationalism or separatism has to the black radical today. All the points stress the establishment of truly black communities.

Black nationalism

"Black power is nationalization. Absolute control of resources beneficial to a national group. It cannot come to exist in areas of white control."[35] This neatly expresses the concern of many black radicals today: Is liberation possible in racist America? The answer is clearly becoming No because racism cannot be overcome within the current system.

The tenth point of the Black Panther Party Platform puts it well: "We want land, bread, housing, education, clothing, justice, and peace. And as our major political objective, a United Nations-

---

[35] Le Roi Jones, "The Need for a Cultural Base to Civil Rites & Bpower Mooments," Barbour (ed.), p. 121.

supervised plebiscite to be held throughout the black colony in which only black colonial subjects will be allowed to participate for the purpose of determining the will of black people as to their national destiny."[36]

There is little more that can be said. The point is clear and simple. Blacks assert: We are a colony, and we demand our freedom. Even where the demand is employed as a symbol of oppression rather than a desired political end, the point is the same: "Let my people go." We are oppressed; we demand our freedom. We demand the right to life, liberty, and property.

Black radicals now believe that oppression cannot be ended as long as the American system remains as it is. "It is clear that America as it now exists must be destroyed. There is no other way."[37] Revolution becomes more attractive as reform fails.

The recognition of blackness as good combined with the demand for black control of black communities leads almost inevitably to demands for separatism. And the concepts of community and equality are also linked to separatism. A commune system can include black communes—the ultimate of black control of black communities.

The black radicals have split from the white radicals, but they all agree on the basic goals. The black radicals have told the white radicals to get out of the ghettos and let us run our own communities, but the differences between black and white are not very deep. Running your own communities is a fundamental postulate of the New Left. The notion of separation can thus be seen to be directly related to the New Left idea of community, and there are other basic relationships between the New Left and black radicalism, such as (1) concern with the problem of alienation and the search for the authentic self; (2) equality; and

---

[36] "Black Panther Party Platform and Program: What We Want, What We Believe (October, 1966)," in Philip S. Foner (ed.), *The Black Panthers Speak* (Philadelphia: J. B. Lippincott, 1970), p. 3.

[37] Julius Lester, *Look Out, Whitey! Black Power's Gon' Get Your Mama!* (New York: Dial Press, 1968), p. 137.

(3) liberty. Those who emphasize the differences are wrong. The differences exist, and while they may be fatal if stressed too much, they are much less significant than the similarities.

The problem of tactics

Black radicals and the rest of the New Left divide primarily over three points. The first, the need for the blacks to take care of their own communities, has already been mentioned. The second, the problem of tactics, needs to be specified more fully here. Due to their experiences in the ghettos, their treatment by American society, and their perceptions of the depth of racism in this society, black radicals view the possibilities of change significantly differently than do white radicals.

Black radicals, although they believe in revolution and feel that ultimately it will be necessary, also believe that white radicals who accept the possibility of revolution in the near future are naïve. Black radicals argue that the forces opposed to revolution are tremendously more powerful than the forces that favor revolution. For the black, at least, the system has always been willing to suppress or kill anyone who favors change and works actively for it. The white radical has never experienced the degree of suppression that a typical black man experiences in his day-to-day life.

Therefore, the black radical argues that we must separate the movements so that the black is not drawn into stupid moves that the naïve white takes. Because revolution is not possible today, it is necessary to carefully organize and develop a revolutionary force for the future within the ghetto. Also, the black radical must spend a significant amount of time on questions of immediate reform, due to conditions that exist in the ghetto.[38]

The third difference between black radicals and the New Left, the different emphasis on the type of governmental control of the economy in the future is not very important now, but it may

---

[38] See, for example, the section entitled "Community Activities" in Foner (ed.), op. cit., pp. 167–81.

become important later. ". . . we cannot end racism, capitalism, colonialism and imperialism until the reins of state power are in the hands of those who understand that the wealth, the total wealth of any country and the world, belongs equally to all people."[39] The difference is in the concern with "state power" by Brown and other black radicals. Having faced "state power," they do not see it disappearing after the revolution, as do many of the rest of the New Left. This could become a major area of conflict. It has separated radical groups for over a century now.

But the most important thing is that the blacks feel the need of getting their own people together and developing a sense of black consciousness, a sense of black community. In addition, they are attempting to develop black leadership in the black community that does not accept a back seat to whitey. The black radical is concerned with overcoming Uncle Tomism and developing black power in black communities today, even though he believes that the system must be overthrown.

Blacks must arm so that they can no longer be suppressed by whitey in their daily life. They must fight back now wherever possible against whitey. The tactics of the urban guerilla apply most specifically to the black in the ghetto. The black faces the suppression of the system daily on his own turf. He knows the ghetto better than any white policeman or army officer ever will. He is part of the black community and can fade into it and will almost always be supported by the community.

The black radical will strike back at the system and its representatives, particularly the police, wherever and whenever it is possible. The bottled-up hatred of the system simply will not wait for the revolution that may not come in his lifetime. He will strike out today against the system and kill a policeman—"Off a pig." "In order to stop the slaughter of the people, we must accelerate the slaughter of the pigs."[40] And, he will try to reform the

---

[39] Brown, p. 128.

[40] Eldridge Cleaver, "On Weatherman," in Harold Jacobs (ed.), *Weatherman* (Np.: Ramparts Press, Inc., 1970), p. 295.

system in the ghetto. White reforms in black ghettos can never satisfy him. Black reforms in black ghettos are the only possible ways of reforming the ghettos.

The black man and black woman must be allowed to develop their own sense of identity, their own community organization and their own feeling of community, and they must have black power. This entails, to some extent, a demand by all black radicals and many black reformers for separation, or black control of black areas, today.

The Women's Liberation Movement[41]

In its broadest, most inclusive sense, the Women's Liberation Movement is the struggle for a social revolution resulting in a more humane society, one where everyone will be able to reach their fullest potential as a human being, no longer thwarted by "role-playing." The Women's Liberation Movement shares with other New Left groups the concepts of participatory democracy, equality, liberty, and community but the approach to these ideas makes this Movement stand apart from male-dominated New Left groups. Because full participation of both men and women will be necessary to form a free and healthy society, the Women's Liberation Movement firmly believes that the elimination of sexism is essential first. To destroy sexist attitudes is no easy task. Women are discovering every day how deeply ingrained it is. Ellen Willis puts it well: "Femaleness like blackness is a biological fact, a fundamental condition. Like racism, male supremacy permeates all strata of this society. And it is even more deeply entrenched. Whites are at least defensive about racism; men including most radicals, black and white—are proud of their chauvanism."[42]

Frances Beal, a black woman, states the importance of sexism to maintaining this society: "Much in the same way the poor white

---

[41] This section was written by Linda Lewis and Sally Baideme.

[42] Ellen Willis, "Liberation Forum," *The Guardian*, February 15, 1969 (reprint, p. 1).

cracker in the South, who is equally victimized, looks down upon blacks and contributes to the oppression of blacks—so by giving to men a false feeling of superiority (at least in their own home or in their relationships with women)—the oppression of women acts as an escape for capitalism."[43]

Social equality

Differences are certainly a mark of the Women's Liberation Movement—from city to city and, indeed, within cities. Working-class women, black and white, have different needs from professional and nonworking-class women. Black women face certain problems which white women do not share, and white women have been a party to the racist attitudes and repression felt by their black sisters. It is therefore important to women's liberation for *all women* to look at these attitudes, overcome them, and learn in what ways this society has exploited and intentionally divided *all women.*

Women are beginning to recognize and understand these barriers. For instance, when black working-class women face white working-class women, they must first work through the racism that has separated them and then deal with their common problems as working-class women. Debbie D'Amico, a white woman, has pointed out that racism among working-class women has kept them from recognizing that the rich and powerful were unwilling to raise their salaries simply because it would cut into profits, not because people, black and white, didn't deserve it. "We believed black people were so inferior that they weren't supposed to make it—we believed we were superior and could make it—but we never did and we blame ourselves."[44]

Some differences exist in the Women's Liberation Movement because of differing life styles or approaches among women. There

---

[43] Frances M. Beal, "Double Jeopardy: To Be Black and Female," in Robin Morgan (ed.), p. 345. © 1970, Frances M. Beal.

[44] Debby D'Amico, "To My White Working-Class Sisters," *Up From Under,* Vol. 1 (August/September 1970), p. 17.

are struggles between "straight" women and their lesbian sisters in trying to understand, accept each other, and work together for the liberation of all women. "A woman who is totally independent of men—who obtains love, sex, and self-esteem from other women —is a terrible threat to male supremacy. She doesn't need them, and therefore they have less power over her."[45] The fear of homosexuality is often used by society to prevent an understanding of the deeper causes of oppression. Therefore, the fact that some women have consciously chosen the companionship of other women for their emotional, sexual, and intellectual needs and that they can lead normal and productive lives without men is both enlightening and frightening to most women. Necessary work in the movement could be crippled by an unwillingness to accept different life styles such as the lesbian relationship; therefore discussion groups have been started between gay and straight women so that they can understand how lesbianism has been used to divide women. This then puts the issue in a more accurate perspective.

Women Liberationists believe that as women really begin to understand and respect one another, through sharing and analyzing the personal experiences of other women, they will gain insight into their "caste" position in society. By unconsciously accepting this role, women have helped to maintain a system which is oppressive to all—children, women, and men. Women are now struggling to acquire this understanding and to join together in attacking, questioning, and attempting to change the institutions and attitudes that oppress and exploit them. Through boycotts, demonstrations, and sit-ins, women are saying No or asking why and expecting an answer. Books and pamphlets are being written by women examining the history of women and its relations to women's position in today's society. All of these efforts are producing a radical feminist politics.

---

[45] Martha Shelley, "Notes of a Radical Lesbian," in Morgan (ed.), p. 308.

Because of the deeply ingrained belief that women are inferior, a very large percentage of women involved in Women's Liberation know that even if a capitalist society were replaced by a more humane society under socialism this would not guarantee the liberation of women. This is illustrated by the attitude of many New Left groups which champion socialism, towards women's liberation. Even though the New Left and Women's Liberation share common ideas for creating a better society, it does not mean that most New Left groups are more willing to give women an equal share in decision-making. Nor are they willing to help to change the male/female roles and relationships. While the male-dominated New Left groups seem to have tacitly accepted Women's Liberation, they attempt to manipulate women into using women's issues as an organizing tool for their goals. And they use guilt to put the women's issue as secondary to "The Movement"—that is, "What makes you think you're more oppressed than black people, you white middle-class chick."[46]

New Left rhetoric is filled with praise of equality, but for women this means that her value still depends on her looks and "her man" and his importance in the group. Marge Piercy, in "The Grand Coolie Damn" describes the reaction to a woman speaking at a meeting ". . . she had read her texts and had a militant Left position and an obvious sense of style." The result was that "She had no impact." She goes on to say the woman's chances would have been better "if she had been sexually connected with any of the *machers* present . . . for she would have been automatically present at the small caucuses and meetings where policy, unfortunately, originates."[47]

One major point of difference between the Women's Liberation Movement and the New Left is that male-dominated New Left groups have organized themselves in the same way that

---

[46] Barbara Burris, et al., "Fourth World Manifesto" (Detroit, Mich.: Women-Fourth World, 1971), p. 11. Mimeographed paper.

[47] Marge Piercy, "The Grand Coolie Damn," in Morgan (ed.), pp. 428–29.

groups have always organized—through a power and leadership hierarchy and appointed spokesmen. In male-dominated New Left groups it seems a person is still valued by the kind of work he or she does. If you are stapling leaflets or washing coffee cups rather than speaking or writing, there is very little chance that your ideas or opinions will carry much weight in policy-making. Men in the New Left will not accept a woman who can argue, question, analyze any more than men in the rest of society will —woman's place remains the same: supportive, adoring, and quiet.

Contemporary radical feminists, on the other hand, have consciously avoided building hierarchical structures into their organizations. In the Women's Liberation Movement all women share in the drudge work and the making of policy. There are no formal leaders or spokeswomen. As the Women's Liberation Movement has grown and gained interest, speakers bureaus have been set up with a coordinator and group of speakers that change regularly so that more women can have the experience of speaking before groups. Workshops are held so that new women can learn from the experience of others familiar with speaking to large audiences and many times they will go to meetings in pairs, one experienced and the other new so that confidence can be built up and passed on to others. When representatives are needed for regional or international meetings, volunteers are usually sent or an individual is randomly selected from among those who are interested in such meetings. This flexibility is possible because of a confidence that all women are capable of making decisions, carrying out actions, and forming policy.

Community

The nuclear family is the primary and most accepted life style. This produces isolated competitive units, and it is the main institution perpetuating sex roles. The harm and inflexibility of this life style has been recognized by the Women's Liberation Movement and the New Left. This is one of the main reasons for the stress on communal living and community as a method to "help us learn about ourselves and about better ways of living."[48] Alternative living arrangements, however, are not the totality of political action but rather an important part of carrying on political work. As one editorial stated, "Any decision to begin a new life style now must be accompanied by real struggles to free the majority of people to be able to choose how and with whom they will live."[49]

Many women involved in the Women's Liberation Movement have formed all-women communes; and there are women's centers in various cities which serve as temporary communities where women can stay and associate with others who share basic ideas and feelings and can receive needed counseling, such as that regarding legal questions or abortion. And these centers serve as a place where a woman can rest and think during an uprooted period in her life.

The communes and centers serve as places which supply the support and security necessary when someone starts to perceive their life differently and/or begins to change it. The communities and centers allow ideas to be exchanged, problems shared and analyzed, and strategies for dealing with these problems or regarding specific actions or demonstrations worked out.

Some of these communities are work collectives which center around a particular aspect of the movement such as a newspaper, journal, crafts, theater, rock bands or a specific issue such as women and health, women and day care, or women and the war. These collectives not only allow women to act out a personal life style but to integrate their work *into* that life style. In other words, a woman doesn't have to live in a commune and only be part of and involved with the Movement on evenings and weekends while spending forty hours a week doing deadening work that requires compromising her beliefs. Many mixed and all-women

---

[48] "Editorial," *Women: A Journal of Liberation,* Vol. 2 (Winter 1971), p. 1.

[49] Ibid., p. 65.

communes arrange jobs so that they can survive economically. For example, in some, everyone may work part-time, or some may work full-time and support the rest during part of the year and the others work full-time during the rest of the year so that all can devote full-time to the movement at some point during the year.

Some women involved in the Women's Liberation Movement live in mixed communes and try to change the roles and relationships between men and women, parents and children, and with other women within these circumstances. In some mixed communes, the people involved take part in raising all the children who are part of the living situation. Therefore, the major responsibility no longer falls on the two parents, especially the mother. Many of the children raised in a commune also take part in community schools or day-care centers, which allows them to interact with their peers in a relaxed atmosphere not hampered by rigid rules. This also provides for their exposure to more adults, both male and female. Through these situations, the child has a variety of experiences and learns from a variety of personalities. Since he/she sees both men and women doing the same things, the typical early socialization that "what little boys do is this, and what little girls do is that" is less likely to take place. This situation allows the parents, especially the woman to relate to the child in a more relaxed and healthy way because she no longer has sole responsibility for raising the child.

However, while the New Left and Women's Liberation share many goals in advocating communal living and in building alternative institutions, such as free clinics, food co-ops, and day-care centers, the fact is that women's time in far too many of these mixed communities is spent in traditional ways—cooking, cleaning, washing dishes, child care, typing, stapling, or providing sex on demand ("You're a liberated woman, aren't you").[50] The

---

[50] For example, see William Hedgepeth and Dennis Stock, *The Alternative: Communal Life in New America* (New York: The Macmillan Company, 1970), p. 74.

number of tales of horror and degradation from women in these New Left communes and communities is staggering.[51]

Beverly Jones has a suggestion for future communities so that women can be freed from such "chores" and can spend more of their time as they choose. "Houses might be built around schools to be rented only to people with children enrolled in the particular school, and only as long as they were enrolled."[52] She points out that these communities could include many services such as nurseries, cheap or cooperative cafeterias, and space for group activities; for example, classes in self-defense. In such communities, individual women would not be solely responsible for their own family's meal preparation, childcare, and housework. It is essential, Jones points out, to have such projects so that women can be free to discover themselves and take part in the movement. She continues, saying, "And the projects themselves, by freeing a woman's time and placing her in innumerable little ways into more of a position of equality, will go a long way toward restructuring the basic marital and parental relationships."[53]

Most women in the Women's Liberation Movement still live in the nuclear family situation, but they can still be part of women's communities. The small, consciousness-raising group helps to create a feeling of community and helps to provide the support needed by each individual. The small group can create an atmosphere where common needs are met by the group, where feelings are expressed and thoughts exchanged and closeness and trust are developed. Many groups, after a period of getting to know each other, discover that some women in the group have immediate problems that need to be solved before they are free to spend time analyzing and understanding the broader reasons for their oppression as women. Some of these problems deal with

---

[51] For example, see Vivian Estellachild, pp. 40–43.

[52] Part I, Beverly Jones and Judith Brown, *Toward a Female Liberation Movement* (Boston: New England Free Press, 1968?), p. 17.

[53] Ibid.

the family, and care of children and the home, "duties" which leave her struggling alone to find time for herself; some concern employment, finding a job or dealing with an oppressive on-the-job situation. Alternative solutions can be found by the group. One woman explains the importance of this approach to an individual's problems as, "A method in itself revolutionary; a way of breaking down one of the strongest bulwarks of our society—the belief that an individual's perceptions of herself cannot be understood by anyone else; that individual problems must, therefore, be dealt with in isolation and loneliness."[54] The sense of community becomes very real through the small group. It becomes possible to relate openly and become involved in a constructive way. Through this process, women develop self-respect —their ideas and thoughts are worth relating to others. And they also develop respect for their sisters. An entirely new world opens up as they create a new approach to life and begin to integrate this approach into their daily lives. Alone, most women would probably not have attempted to change their lives.

There are many stages a small group goes through, and each group is different, but if the women involved deal with each other honestly, there can develop a positive, highly-motivating situation, and learning can take place both by formulating and testing theories that are important to all women and by relating directly to others.

Participatory democracy

The importance of direct participation in decisions relating to your life and the lives of those around you has been consistently stressed by the New Left. Women, however, discovered that direct participation did not apply to them. They were still expected to take a back seat. Beverly Jones points out that both the black

---

[54] Ronnie Lichtman et al., "Consciousness Raising, Sisterhood, and the Small Group (1970)," p. 1. Mimeographed paper.

militant and the white radical were helped by the separation of
the movement into two parts. ". . . the best thing that may yet
happen to potentially radical young women is that they will be
driven out of both of these groups. That they will be forced to
stop fighting for the 'movement' and start fighting primarily for
the liberation and independence of women."[55]

If the concepts of equality and liberty had applied to everyone
in the New Left groups, participation by women in decision-
making would have been the logical step. Male chauvinism, however, is deeply ingrained. Although some New Left men are beginning to look at their own chauvinism, women are no longer
willing to wait until men say, "OK, we are ready to give you the
right to participate"; women are taking that right *now*. They are
taking action, formulating programs, and making the decisions
that are relevant to their lives and their oppression; they are not
passively waiting for decisions to be handed to them.

To participate directly in decision-making is an exhilarating
feeling and an important step in personal growth and collective
thinking. The importance of an atmosphere that enables women
who have never before expressed themselves politically to do so
is not easily understood, particularly by men. Women have become so used to a definite structure and leaders (mostly men) to
guide them that at first there is often a strong doubt that their
opinions are valid or worth hearing. And functioning without
leaders is also difficult at first. But, in time, through personal
struggle and with the support of other sisters, women begin to
feel the value of their opinions. Ideas are shared with other
women, receiving support and criticism from them rather than
receiving approval from some "leader." The important point is
that a person can participate without being stifled by leaders or
being judged by the kind of work she performs in the movement.
Martha Shelley points out the importance of all people being able

---

[55] Beverly Jones, p. 3.

to share, criticize, and learn from each others' ideas. "She struggles for understanding and pays attention to an idea rather than to the source of the idea. An idea is not correct simply because it issues from the mouth of Mao or Che or any other leader."[56]

All women have the ability to make decisions, be creative, and to recognize that each woman's personal experience must be taken into account in every decision. Further, since the ultimate goal is a completely cooperative and equal society, our organizations must reflect that now. Direct participation is not as smooth running or as "efficient" as a structured hierarchical process, because it requires flexibility and a willingness to struggle to understand the many positions on particular issues or problems. Only in this way can the policy decided upon be the fairest and most inclusive. To say that it has been and is still difficult is an understatement. Women's Liberation groups often find themselves in a state of disarray and factionalism because there is no one leader to guide the way. However, in the larger society where the few control and determine decisions, the outcome is seldom beneficial to those directly concerned, even though the process may be more efficient. Our "efficient" system has gotten us gross inequality of the races and sexes, an alien, inhuman, technological society, destruction of the environment, and never-ending war.

Direct involvement in decisions has created the best possible learning situation for women to develop and analyze ideas, and with this new insight and knowledge women have gained the confidence to act. Regional conferences or planning meetings for nationwide action such as Women's Strike Day, August 26th, and International Women's Day, March 8th, as well as local meetings concerning the internal workings of local Women's Liberation offices and centers have all been genuine attempts to put the concept of participatory democracy to a test. After these

---

[56] Martha Shelley, "Subversion in the Women's Movement, What is to be Done," *Off Our Backs,* Vol. 1 (November 8, 1970), p. 7.

meetings/conferences the newspapers of the women's movement carry articles analyzing what went on and differing viewpoints are expressed. This, then, offers the opportunity for all concerned to find out what happened, analyze the dynamics, and apply what was learned to future actions or to solving more immediate problems.

Alternative institutions have been established that meet the immediate needs of women. Day-care centers, community schools, abortion counseling, health care are examples. These have been founded by women (in some cases with men participating), and they are places where participatory democracy is put to the test. The experience of one D.C. day-care center clearly points this out. They have tried to operate on the basis of consensus through "ongoing discussions" rather than votes or rules. "We have always hoped to relate to each other in an open, honest way that is supportive. This always involves the very difficult tasks of really listening to each other, trying to understand each other, being tolerant of where others are at, and still expressing and working for what you think is correct."[57]

Women are willing to work together and create necessary alternative institutions which meet their needs. The fact that this is a slow and ongoing process is positive not negative—too many long-lived institutions in our society fail to meet the needs they are supposed to meet. These institutions often exploit the very people they were set up to help, and they are unwilling to have them share in the decisions that control their lives. There is a humanness, a warmth, and an aliveness in this new process which allows for growth, learning, and solutions that are relevant to the problems of the people involved.

The struggle will continue, because if equality and a more humane society is to be achieved, that achievement must *begin*

---

[57] Marcia and Norma, "The Children's House," *Off Our Backs,* Vol. 1 (February 12, 1971), p. 9.

now. And, in fact, important results have already been achieved—both in the increase in the number of women who have begun to assert themselves and see themselves as worthwhile human beings, and in the influence Women's Liberation has already had on the society at large.

6

PARTICIPATORY DEMOCRACY

In each chapter so far I have touched on topics related to participatory democracy (familiarly known as *p.d.*). Participatory democracy has often been thought of as the most original contribution of the New Left to political thought, but whether or not it is truly original (it isn't)[1] is not really important. It is a basic part of New Left thought.

Its significance is twofold: (1) It is a basic political goal of all New Left groups, and (2) it is a principle of organization within most New Left groups. Both as a basic goal and as a current principle of organization it is seen as:

1. The basic method of decision making.
2. The means of political organization within groups and communities.
3. A protection for individual and community equality and ·liberty.
4. Part of the process of the search for the authentic self.

In order to understand how participatory democracy is expected to fill all these roles, it will be necessary to look at the concept in

---

[1] In a recent collection on participatory democracy, the editors included a number of articles from writers of previous centuries. See Terrence E. Cook and Patrick M. Morgan (eds.), *Participatory Democracy* (San Francisco: Canfield Press, 1971).

some detail and compare it with more traditional conceptions of democracy.

Since democracy is a much used word and one with many favorable connotations, it is used to describe many different institutional arrangements. It is applied to the one-party authoritarian people's democracies of the Communist world and similar situations in the developing nations. And it is used to refer to the representative system that exists in most Western countries.[2] The word *democracy* implies rule by the people, and it is this that advocates of participatory democracy hope to establish.

In the Western tradition, democracy clearly refers to an institutional arrangement, such as representatives chosen at periodic elections, that give the citizenry some degree of control over government and governmental policy. The New Left contends that the people are not sufficiently involved in the political process and, therefore, participatory democracy refers to a number of related approaches to achieving greater involvement through more widespread participation by the citizenry. The received tradition and myth of Western democracy includes widespread participation as a desirable but seldom achieved goal. But the specific institutional arrangements for such participation have been the focus of much dispute, and it is the failure, as seen from the New Left, of the current system that participatory democracy is supposed to correct. These failures focus on the inability of the current political system to respond rapidly to the changing needs and desires of the populace. The failure of responsiveness is the main focus of complaint, but combined with this is the perceived failure of the political system to concern itself with the most serious concerns and ideals of youth today. A system of participatory democracy should reflect the wishes of the people.

---

[2] See the discussion in C. B. Macpherson, *The Real World of Democracy* (Oxford: Clarendon Press, 1966) for an introduction to the diversity of "democracies."

The concept

The basic characteristics of participatory democracy are found in the "Port Huron Statement" of 1962.

As a social system we seek the establishment of a democracy of individual participation, governed by two central aims: that the individual share in those social decisions determining the quality and direction of his life; that society be organized to encourage independence in men and provide the media for their common participation.[3]

This statement sketches in the basic characteristics, but clearly it is not complete enough for a thorough understanding. Under our current system of government an individual is represented in the legislative, executive, and judicial functions of government by another individual. Participatory democracy either would replace this system with one in which each individual would represent himself and no one else, or, in its most conservative formulations, add an additional level of government.

Looking first at the more radical formulation, it can be seen in the decision-making process of a contemporary commune. In the evening, after the work of the day is finished, the members of the commune come together to discuss the affairs of the commune. In this meeting, in which everyone participates with an equal voice, all the decisions are made that affect the commune members. Of course the workings of such a formulation would be much more complicated in a larger society, but the basic idea can best be seen in the context of a small community.

Participatory democracy is used not only for making decisions, but also for enforcing decisions, and for adjudicating disputes. If necessary, the entire community acts to enforce the decisions, but the burden of obedience is left on the individual. Since each individual participated in making the decision, it is *his* decision and, therefore, it is expected that each individual will simply accept the

---

[3] "Port Huron Statement," in Jacobs and Landau, op. cit., p. 155.

decision and not require external pressure. But if external pressure is necessary, it is provided by the community as a whole. At the same time, if an individual is unwilling to follow the decision, it is likely that the commune would reconsider it first with the full participation of the recalcitrant member who would then be able to explain his position and attempt to gain community support for a change. It is assumed that disputes would not arise after decisions had been made through the process of participatory democracy. And since everyone participates in making decisions, each individual will be deeply concerned and intimately involved in attempting to resolve any dispute. In a closely-knit community, ties of friendship and love should smooth over most disputes. But if the dispute is not smoothed over by discussion within the community combined with the ties of friendship and love, it will probably be assumed that the community made an error in the original decision.

This is a functioning commune operating on the basis of participatory democracy. It shows participatory democracy basically as a system by which everyone in a group participates directly in making the decisions that affect their lives, in enforcing such decisions, and in adjudicating disputes. Also, it can be seen that adequate functioning of participatory democracy depends in large part on the adequate functioning of the community system. It should be clear that community and participatory democracy also depend upon equality and liberty to function adequately. For participatory democracy and community to work, each individual must feel himself to be equal to every other individual within the community and free to express himself or herself. A community cannot function unless all individuals in it feel equal and free to express themselves.

The basic idea behind participatory democracy is "Power to the People." This is an axiom of New Left thought; it is not based upon any other presuppositions about the value of power to the people; it is based primarily on the acknowledgement that the present system does not work as it should and that a more authoritarian system would be even worse. Although there are a few exceptions to these statements, the exceptions do not represent the main thrust of New Left thought. It is assumed without argument that a system operating on the basis of power held by individuals to control their own lives is better than any other system. Attempts to get behind this argument to theoretical explanations of the advantages of participation will almost always go wrong. Although there is some recognition that participation adds to the ability of individuals to recognize themselves and thus participate more fully and more adequately, this is not seen as a reason for participatory democracy, but simply a good effect of it.

The forms

Participatory democracy is a general idea that can take many forms in practice. The New Left holds that the appropriate forms must evolve out of the needs of a specific group at a specific time and place—no generalizations regarding forms should be considered entirely valid. At the same time, it is possible to suggest some of the directions that participatory democracy has taken so far that have gained fairly wide acceptance. I shall look at three of these. One, consensus, relates to the operation of participatory democracy within groups. The second, decentralization, relates to the modification of the political and economic system suggested by the theme of participatory democracy. The third, workers' control, is a specific case of decentralization that helps to understand the proposed economic system. Other specific forms of decentralization, such as student power, will also be touched on briefly. In addition, I shall discuss some of the more conservative alternative forms that participatory democracy might take that have been suggested by various people.

Consensus

In all the specific forms in which the concept of participatory democracy might be worked out, the key element is found in consensus. Consensus means the consideration of an issue and the discussion of the decision until all agree or until the disagreements are over matters that the minority considers unimportant.

A procedure using consensus requires that the individual members be dedicated to the purposes of the group, that is, that they have a sense of community; it requires equality and liberty; and it requires a lot of time. One example of participatory democracy working on the basis of consensus is the following:

At an Underground Press meeting, the "hippies" (correlation of the early christians) sat around in a circle and spoke in turn, arbitrarily. No procedure was followed. Some spoke articulately, others stupidly and irrelevantly. Eventually the most articulate and intelligent were heard and evolved as natural leaders rising to meet the occasion. After the particular event had been dealt with they sank back to enrich the mass, so to speak . . . not consolidating power or looking to secure a selfish personal control over the group.[4]

This example illustrates both the process of participatory democracy in one situation and points to the problem of leadership within it.

Consensus is one of those unfortunate words that have been used too freely to describe something that it not included in the original term. Consensus is best thought of as an agreement which develops or aggregates from below. It should not include any notion of an agreement imposed upon from above, even if such an agreement is later accepted by the group. Consensual agreement does not, in fact, even include any notion of an "above" that · could impose an agreement.

Consensual agreement is compatible with the notions of community, liberty, and equality that are conditioning factors for the existence of participatory democracy. It may be the only form that is so compatible. It works best in a small, tightly-knit group or community that is composed of individuals who consider themselves free and are secure in that freedom and thus do not feel a

---

[4] Walter Bowart and Allen Katzman, "Sgt. Pepper's Political Club and Band," *The East Village Other,* July 1, 1967, quoted in Kornbluth (ed.), op. cit., p. 190.

need to conform to someone else's position. The desire for agreement will come out of respect for and agreement with the goals of the group and respect for the other members of the group. This requires, in addition to the freedom of each individual, that each individual sees himself as the equal of every other individual within the group. It does not mean that he sees himself as an individual who is necessarily as articulate or as intelligent as everyone else, but he must not see himself as inherently inferior or inherently superior to any of the members in the group. If anyone feels this way, it will make the development of consensus much more difficult, if not impossible. Equality in this sense can best be seen in a feeling of acceptance as a valuable member of the group or community. All the members must have this feeling.

If these conditions are met, or at least approximated, it is possible to envision consensual agreement functioning quite well. Individuals sit around, preferably in a circle so that each person can communicate directly with every other person in the group, and begin to discuss the questions that are bothering the group or some individual within the group. Any question can be brought up. There is no agenda and no formal procedure. Each person freely speaks his mind on whatever issues concern him. The group discusses, reasons, and argues, and either reaches a general agreement or continues the discussion at a future meeting until a general agreement can be reached. It is important that no member be strongly opposed to the conclusion reached. It is certainly possible that a member will not agree with all of the details of a particular conclusion, but he must not believe that these details are extremely significant. If even one individual feels strongly opposed to the agreement, the decision should be put off until all can be convinced of the rightness of a decision. It is important that the group be willing to leave questions open until all can agree with a solution rather than closing off debate on the basis of a vote. Majority rule is not the process of consensual agreement—50 percent plus one does not make a decision; only 100 percent makes the decision.

Decentralization

While consensus may be the future method of decision-making within communities, this still leaves the problem of the structure of the political and economic systems. The most important concept relevant to structure is decentralization. Staughton Lynd sees three roles that decentralization plays.

1. A vision of a future society which would be both socialist and humane;
2. An ideology of resistance to big business and big government;
3. A method of struggle comparable to guerilla movements in underdeveloped nations or to the European resistance movements during World War II.[5]

Although Lynd can be faulted for implying that the concept is of more importance than it really is for the New Left, his distinctions are useful as a way of approaching discussion of the concept.

Looking first at the vision of the future society, decentralization does play an important role. The New Left argues against utopias, but it is still possible to construct a definite, fairly clear vision of a desired future society from the various writers, particularly those in the underground papers. One must envision a society in which the large metropolitan areas that exist now have disappeared. Instead, there are many small towns surrounded by agricultural areas. Each town would combine agriculture, crafts, and light industry. Living arrangements would vary considerably from community to community, but they would be designed to encourage face-to-face contacts and heightened interpersonal relations, while insuring the possibility of privacy.[6] The urban area has been broken up—society is decentralized. This totally transformed environment is one aspect of the vision of the future found

---

[5] Staughton Lynd, "Decentralization: A Road to Power," *Liberation*, 12 (May-June 1967), p. 32.

[6] An interesting, albeit somewhat idiosyncratic, discussion of similar ideas can be found in E. A. Gutkind, *The Expanding Environment: The End of Cities—The Rise of Communities* (London: Freedom Press, 1953).

in parts of the New Left, but it is one upon which there is significant disagreement. But it is still one of the visions, and it is the most thoroughgoing expression of decentralization.

But this is a vision of the far future and, although it may be seen as an ultimate goal, it is not an immediate goal. In a more immediate sense, decentralization means a redistribution of political and economic power. The slogan "Power to the People" means that political power should go directly to the small communities that exist today within larger metropolitan areas. In this sense it does not necessarily mean that power should go directly to the people. Political power should be removed from current governmental structures and placed more directly in the hands of the people within small communities or neighborhoods through neighborhood associations and the like.

An expression of this notion can be seen in the following petition that was put on the ballot as a proposed amendment to the city charter of Oakland, California:

87 (s) *Establishment of Separate Police Departments:* For the purpose of providing police services to the people of the city of Oakland, there are established two police departments, one for each of the two Districts in which the City is divided as hereinafter set forth and described.

87 (d) *Neighborhood Divisions:* Each Police Department is divided into five neighborhood Divisions described below . . .

87 (f) *Police Council:* Each Neighborhood Division shall be divided into fifteen Police Council Precincts by the City Clerk; the population of each such Precinct is not to exceed any other Precinct by more than ten percent of the population of the entire District divided by the number of Precincts therein. The registered voters in each Precinct shall elect a Police Councilman who will serve in that capacity for a term of two years, unless recalled.

87 (L) *Duties of Council:* The Neighborhood Council shall, within ten days of its own election, select a Commissioner. In addition to selection of Commissioners, the Councils shall review the policies of the Police Department and recommend changes or modifications of such policies when such policies

no longer reflect the needs or will of the populace in the
Neighborhood represented by the Council.
91   *Residence:* All Police officers shall reside in the area covered
by the department they work for.[7]

This amendment to the Oakland City Charter reflects one level of
decentralization—neighborhood control of the services that effect
them. The relationship here between decentralization and participatory democracy should be obvious. By placing control of the
police department in the hands of the people in a specific neighborhood, it is assumed that the police will be more responsive to
the needs of the community. The police are more likely to develop
good relations with the people in the community, and both the
police and the members of the community are more likely to respect each other. In some ways, this is an attempt to return to the
popular image of the policeman as a friend that was supposedly
held when the policeman lived in the neighborhood, walked a
beat, became acquainted with the people in the neighborhood,
and in general could be seen as part of the neighborhood. The
image of policemen riding by twos in patrol cars, living outside
the neighborhood, being of different color or ethnic background,
and in general separate from the cares and needs of the community is being attacked.

This was an attempt to practice decentralization. Although the
amendment failed, it does state some of the desires of those who
favor decentralization and participatory democracy. Another example is the attempt, in parts of New York City, to bring neighborhood schools under the control of the people of the neighborhood.[8] In this case there was an attempt to take local schools out
of the control of a board of education that represented a large

---

[7] "Petition for Submission to Electors of Proposed Amendment to the
City Charter of Oakland." Parts of this petition have been reprinted in
Cook and Morgan (eds.), pp. 428–31, under the title "Black Panthers
Petition for Neighborhood Control of the Police."

[8] See Maurice R. Berube and Marilyn Gittell (eds.), *Confrontation at
Ocean Hill-Brownsville: The New York School Strikes of 1968* (New
York: Praeger, 1969).

metropolis and put it in the hands of the people who lived in the area immediately surrounding the school—particularly those with children in the school. It was assumed that these people would be much more directly aware of the needs of their children and the problems of their neighborhood. This particular experiment ran into serious difficulties with teachers' unions and with various levels of government, and it pointed out that decentralization is not easy to put into practice.

This case showed that other needs and desires have to be taken into account in addition to those of the parents and the children. Specifically there was the problem of teachers who felt threatened by the change, and there was also the difficulty that both the neighborhood people and the teachers wanted complete control of the situation, with no interference from the other group. These groups had been taught and they assumed that having political power is desirable, and they were unwilling to relinquish any part of that power in an attempt to cooperate with others.

Workers' control[9]

A further specific example that is particularly important to, but not yet fully developed by, the New Left is workers' control. Workers' control is decentralization specifically applied to the economy. It is again an expression of the concept, "Power to the People." Those who favor workers' control contend that the work situation must be under the control of the workers. This contention is based in part upon the assumption of the value of participatory democracy, and it is seen as part of the process of over-

---

[9] Workers' control has been a goal of certain parts of anarchism for many years, and it has been practiced on various occasions. Therefore, there is a vast literature on the subject. See, for example, Ken Coates and Tony Topham (eds.), *Workers' Control; A Book of Readings and Witnesses for Workers' Control* (London: Panther Books, 1970); Paul Blumberg, *Industrial Democracy: The Sociology of Participation* (London: Constable, 1968); Hugh Clegg, *A New Approach to Industrial Democracy* (Oxford: Basil Blackwell, 1968); and *Anarchy 2*, Vol. 1 (April 1961), passim for a variety of positions on the subject.

coming alienation. The worker today is believed to be alienated from his work at least in part because he has little or no control over his own working conditions or the operation of the factory. Those who argue for workers' control assert that the worker must take part in controlling the day-to-day functioning of the plant in which he works. He must be directly involved both in the policy-making function that is now almost entirely in the hands of management and in controlling the specific conditions of the shop floor. The power that is now held by management to operate the factory must be taken away from management and given to the workers. Specifically, this means that the workers must be in a position to control production goals and standards, wages, working conditions, and, in general, the entire operation of the plant.

It is assumed that the workers have gained a great deal of knowledge regarding the functioning of the factory on the basis of their work within it. The argument that they should therefore have control over the shop level of the factory is fairly simple. The worker supposedly knows the conditions on the shop floor much better than anyone not daily involved in working there. It is therefore argued that the worker must be free to control his own life in his own specific work situation.

The more complex notion that the worker should control the policy-making level of the factory of course poses more of a question. But here the argument shifts grounds. It is not concerned primarily with the specific working conditions of individual workers or groups of workers; it is concerned with the fact that an elite, management, is given control over policy decisions that affect the lives not only of the workers but the community as a whole, without any mechanism for input by the community. In this sense, workers' control is an attempt to suggest a means by which this elite of management can be replaced by a group whose concerns are not primarily with profit. The workers are assumed to be more concerned with general questions of benefit to the community than would the profit-oriented management.

The specific mechanisms for instituting workers' control at the policy-making level are fairly similar to the suggestions for control of the police department. Management would be chosen by the workers to serve for a specific period of time and would be subject to recall. Before being implemented, all major policy decisions would be presented to the workers as a body so that there would be ample time for discussion. The workers would be able to accept or reject the decision or to let it pass without comment. This would mean that decisions would be made in the open, without secrecy, and with an emphasis on concerns other than profit—concerns related to the benefit to the community as a whole rather than to only one segment of it.

While discussing the economic system, it may be worthwhile to point out that the New Left contains a peculiar ambivalence regarding the complex modern economy. In the first place, the New Left is opposed to the materialism and consumerism that is seen as a result of capitalism and rampant technology. Second, the emphasis on the decentralization of the economy focuses attention on the breakup of large industrial centers and complexes into small industries. Third, the communal movement is representative of a return to the land that has had great appeal to the New Left. But fourth, the New Left seems to accept and encourage the development of automation since it can lead to a leisure-based society. This last belief is not held by everyone in the New Left, but it is certainly held by many. A belief in a leisure-based society through automation is combined with a serious concern with cutting down on unnecessary products and on emphasizing production that is socially useful.[10]

Suggestions for workers' control entail the dismantling of the economic system as it now exists and replacing it with a radically different economic structure. The goals of community benefit,

---

[10] See the various positions in Charles Denby, "Workers Battle Automation," in Long (ed.), pp. 151–71; the various works of Herbert Marcuse; "Meta Information Applications: Technology in a Radical Context (or The Beginnings of a Radical Technology)," in Teodori (ed.), pp. 394–396, and "The Digger Papers: The Post Competition, Comparative Game of a Free City," in Teodori (ed.), p. 379.

popular control, and the decentralization of economic power are the basic assumptions of New Left thought. Workers' control is one specific means of bringing the economy within the framework of participatory democracy. The workers are seen as a surrogate for or representative of direct popular control because they are expected to be the most aware, the most expert, and the most intimately concerned with the functioning of individual factories. But it also illustrates exactly the same difficulties that existed in the experiment in decentralizing educational control. There are many groups concerned with the adequate functioning of the economic system in addition to the workers.

Today decentralization is, in Lynd's terms, "a method of struggle." The slogan "Power to the People" represents both participatory democracy and decentralization. The attempts to give power to the people in such institutions as neighborhood control of police and elementary and high school education, and to give students control of universities are both goals and tactics. A decentralized political and economic structure are both goals of the Movement and in appropriate circumstances specific tactics in an attempt to bring about the more far-reaching goal of revolutionizing the political, economic, and social structures of the country.

Some problems

I have noted two problems with participatory democracy and decentralization in the foregoing—the leadership problem and the coordination or second-level problem. The first of these, the leadership problem, can only be commented on in general terms. It has been noted by some authors[11] that participatory democracy may in fact give rise to exactly what it is attempting to overcome,

---

[11] See, for example, James Eldon and Todd Meyer, "The New Left and Mass Organization: Participatory Democracy vs. Creeping Elitism," unpublished paper presented to the American Political Science Association, September, 1969; and Irving Kristol, "The Old Politics, the New Politics, the New New Politics," *The New York Times Magazine*, November 24, 1968, p. 174.

elitism. In the statement of the operation of an underground press meeting quoted earlier it was noted that during specific meetings leaders arose who were followed during a specific situation and that they then returned to their non-leader role and would not be necessarily a leader in a later specific situation. Again and again the media has created leaders of the Movement, such as Jerry Rubin or Abbie Hoffman or Ti-Grace Atkinson, who may themselves not seek leadership roles.[12] But the Movement is not yet sophisticated enough, at least in all of its manifestations, to avoid following leaders who have been created by the media or who have arisen in specific situations and not returned into the mass. Participatory democracy must have the element of equality in it or it will develop an informal elite which then might become a formal elite. It is quite conceivable that individuals who are very articulate or who have the ability to produce ideas or who have the ability to carry out ideas and put them into a practice will emerge as leaders or as permanent elite through the operation of participatory democracy. In a *Peanuts* cartoon, Charles Schulz has Lucy say that she believes that we are born in squads with one leader and eleven followers. We are so used to the procedure of leadership that unless a community that is attempting to function on the basis of participatory democracy is very aware of the problem, and attempts to overcome it, participatory democracy could easily produce a system in which small groups are in fact one leader and eleven followers rather than twelve free and equal individuals cooperating for mutual benefit.

The second problem, the coordination or second-level problem, can be specified in somewhat more detail. This is the problem of how communities or industries cooperate to organize those areas in which they are mutually interdependent. No community can be entirely self-sufficient and certainly no industry can be. Therefore there must be some way of instituting a level of cooperation

---

[12] See, for example, Rubin, *We Are Everywhere*, pp. 172–74.

above the level of the community or within a factory. This second-level problem has not been directly faced by the New Left.[13] It tends to be assumed that men of goodwill can recognize the mutual benefits resulting from cooperation and can cooperate. But even if this is true, and given the existence of a communal system and intercommunal as well as intracommunal cooperation, it still means that there is need for a level of administration to operate this cooperative enterprise. This does not mean a permanent administrative structure or individuals holding permanent administrative positions, but it does mean that the mechanism of cooperation must be available. And since it is likely that cooperation will be constant, it is probable that some sort of permanent relationship will be established between communes or factories.

This level of administration should be able to operate on participatory democracy like any other level. It is assumed that any individual can be chosen to represent the commune or the factory to such a cooperative body. The individual might be given fairly detailed instructions by the community or the factory or might be assumed to be able to function as a representative of the group without specific directions, due to his intimate knowledge of the group. But the key to the notion is that an individual would serve temporarily as a representative of the group on specific questions subject to review by the group and subject to recall if he in any way violates the desires of the group. This would not be an elective office for a specific term; the person would be chosen to deal with a specific issue with a specific other group or groups. Thus the range of options for the individual would be severely limited, and being subject to constant review and recall the individual should be able to represent his group without too much difficulty.

---

[13] It has been discussed at some length by anarchists. See Peter Kropotkin, *The Conquest of Bread* (New York: G. P. Putnam's Sons, 1907); Kropotkin, *Fields, Factories and Workshops or Industry Combined With Agriculture and Brain Work with Manual Work* (New York: Benjamin Blom, 1968); and C. Berneri, *Peter Kropotkin; His Federalist Ideas* (London: Freedom Press, 1942).

This all assumes a high degree of decentralization and the functioning of participatory democracy, which of course implies equality, liberty, and community. It assumes that men of goodwill, who have been produced by the system, are capable of cooperating with others of different life styles, different belief systems, different languages, and different cultures. It is clear from the mere statement of the assumptions that it cannot be achieved easily. But the argument is not that the answer is simple; it is that our system now is so bad with its competition and its wars, that we must try to establish a system based on cooperation.

Alternative formulations

In the foregoing I have stressed as the New Left position one specific formulation of participatory democracy in which individuals have complete control over their own lives and the political system operates on the basis of consensus. In the Introduction to their collection on participatory democracy, Terrence E. Cook and Patrick M. Morgan suggest four possible formulations of the concept of participatory democracy. These are:

1. A co-determination structure confined to rule-implementation authority;
2. A co-determination structure including rule-making authority;
3. A self-determination structure confined to rule-implementation authority;
4. A self-determination structure including rule-making authority.[14]

It should be clear from the previous discussion that the focus of New Left thought is on the fourth of these models or formulations. At the same time I have noted some of the difficulties of self-determination when more than one group has been involved, and I have suggested that the New Left is willing to accept some forms of co-determination with currently existing governmental bodies as a temporary expedient.

But listing these alternative formulations of participatory de-

---

[14] Cook and Morgan, p. 6.

mocracy to some extent falsifies the basic picture, and an emphasis on the fact that there are a number of alternative models misses the essential point that it is only one model, the fourth, self-control, that is accepted as participatory democracy by the greatest part of the New Left. Any other formulation except this does not represent the central focus of New Left thought on participatory democracy at the present time.

It is likely that in the development of New Left thought and practice some of the other models will be used. For example in the notion of "a co-determination structure including rule-making authority," there is a mechanism for dealing with intercommunity cooperation. This gives the possibility of establishing a means in which communities are equal and cooperatively establish structures for making decisions regarding specific problems that involve more than one community. Thus, although the current formulation of New Left thought on participatory democracy emphasizes the fourth model suggested by Cook and Morgan, it is likely that future thought and practice will focus on some of the other formulations. Some people on the New Left today advocate these more conservative positions either as transitional devices or as current goals, but they do not represent the major focus of New Left thought today.

The specific forms of participatory democracy have yet to be worked out. The New Left is committed to the position that these forms must come out of specific situations dealing with specific issues rather than from rules, regulations, and formulae laid down in advance. In this chapter I have looked at participatory democracy in general and in some of the specific forms that it has taken so far. At this point that is all that can be done.

7

HOW DO WE GET THERE?

I have now presented the basic beliefs, goals, and visions of the New Left. On these points the agreement among individuals and groups is almost complete, even though the practice is not always consistent with the goals. But when we turn to the question posed by the title of this chapter—How do we get there?—agreement disappears. The question of tactics is the most divisive question in the New Left today, and it is splitting a movement whose goals are agreed upon.

The positions range on a continuum that has the hippie or dropout at one end and the professional revolutionary at the other. In between is the "reformer" who thinks that change is possible but that it will take a long time, and the "activist" who is militant but has not dedicated his life to the revolution. Most individuals are a mixture of more than one type, including one (or surprisingly even both) of the two extremes, but there are some individuals who seem to fit only one type—and these individuals are usually found at the extremes.

In this chapter I will look at each of these types in turn, from the hippie or dropout to the professional revolutionary. In each case I will look at the general character of the position and cite some examples.

The hippie

The hippie or dropout is one of the most misunderstood characters of the New Left. He has been over-romanticized by the

115

media; he has been over-sensationalized by the media; and his values and beliefs have been distorted and misunderstood in almost all popular commentary on him. New Left activists, such as Jerry Rubin, see him as follows: "Hippies who've 'dropped out of politics' have dropped out of life, dropped out of their own ability to feel and experience the sufferings of others. Pill-dropping parents escaped to the suburbs; pot smoking hippies escaped to the 'country.' 'No freak will be free until Bobby Seale is free.' "[1] This picture is not entirely inaccurate, certainly, but it is, I believe, important to attempt to understand the hippie approach before judging it.

The Beatnik can be considered a major ancestor of the New Left Movement, and the most direct descendant of the Beatnik is the hippie. The Beatnik had a vision of life as beatific, but his major response to the hassles of life was through the drug of alcohol and later the drug of marijuana. The first drug, alcohol, was a direct response to the despair felt by the Beatnik in that the after-effects of an alcohol high can be quite unpleasant. You suffer with it. Use of marijuana, which came late for the Beatniks, suggested some of the changes in attitudes that the hippies were to bring. The other main response for the Beatnik was sex and this response was carried over by the hippie. But the Beatnik approach, although vague and tending to despair, still had at its base the notion that our society was in terrible condition and that a new society might be founded on love. The "Hippie Movement" today has consisted of a series of attempts to found that new society on love. Haight Ashbury[2] was the first attempt. It was popularized, and by being popularized it was destroyed. The Haight started out as a focus of "flower power"; a society based upon love and

---

[1] Rubin, *We Are Everywhere*, p. 157.

[2] See the following discussions of life in the Haight: "Haight/Hate?" *Communication Company*, August 1967, in Kornbluth (ed.), pp. 247–49; "Mutants Commune," *Berkeley Barb*, August 18, 1967, in ibid., pp. 30–50; and Nicholas von Hoffman, *We Are the People Our Parents Warned Us Against* (Greenwich, Conn.: Fawcett Publications, Inc., 1968).

understanding among the members of the society. It was not based upon an escape from society as it exists today but was an attempt to create a new society without violence, without hate, and without inequality. The media picked up the Haight and it became a magnet for every confused runaway, every dope pusher, every hate-filled person who could make the trip and wear the uniform of the hippie. And the Haight became even more hate-filled than the rest of society. So the hippie left the Haight and joined his brothers and sisters who had been experimenting with life in the country. Thus was founded the new communal movement.

The typical hippie commune is probably the rural commune. It can be characterized as dropout rather than activist, more likely to be thought of as permanent than activist communes, but still very often seen to be temporary.

The problem is not so much the difference between revolution and nonrevolution or even a question of violence versus nonviolence. The hippie certainly believes that contemporary society must be revolutionized and his position on violence is not significantly different from the activist position—he is about as ambivalent. The question comes down to a fundamental disagreement about the possibilities of revolution in contemporary society in the near future. It isn't just this, either, however, because the hippie is more likely to be apolitical than anyone else on the New Left, and hence many are not particularly concerned about the question of when the revolution will come.

The hippie believes either that revolution is impossible or not very likely in the near future, or he does not think in political terms. As a result of this, and the belief that contemporary society is evil and repressive, he chooses to revolt against society by leaving it. The characterization of this revolt by the term "dropout" seems to be fairly accurate. The hippie chooses to leave contemporary society for a different life style that connects little if at all with contemporary society.

This decision to drop out is analogous to, but certainly not the same as, the professional revolutionary's decision to go underground. The hippie, in dropping out, often changes his name to a name of some symbolic importance to him. He breaks virtually all ties with his past and often moves to a part of the country that is unfamiliar to him. He attempts to find a community in which he can live his own life style with a group of people that he can relate to mentally, emotionally, and physically.

He has said to contemporary society that it is so bad that he can no longer support it with his life. This has to be seen as a revolutionary position. Although the hippie is not attempting to overthrow the contemporary system, he is active in demonstrating with his life that he cannot accept contemporary society. The mass of hippies who have gone to the land in the past ten years can be seen as a major demonstration of the failures of contemporary society. There has never been a previous time in which so many youth, of all abilities and backgrounds, have chosen to reject so many of the values that they were brought up with and that their society believes in, and simply leave that society.

Much of the New Left rejects the hippie approach and contends that only by the restructuring of the entire society can any of us be free. They argue that the hippie's "activism" is inadequate because it does not directly attack society.

The hippie's position can be seen in a different light. The hippie is rejecting society by removing himself from it. He is saying that society is not worth attacking. What is important is his life *now* rather than the possibilities of a successful revolution. This is an expression of the apolitical nature of the hippie. He is saying that here and now is important rather than the pie-in-the-sky of revolution. He is saying that dedicating yourself to the possibility of revolution is inadequate; what is important is transforming your own life now. The hippie might argue that he has already won the revolution. Of course there is in that statement a lack of social conscience and a lack of political awareness. But the point still remains that the hippie has in many cases successfully dropped out into a new society and a new life style. He is socially conscious of a new society and he doesn't care about the old society and the people still trapped in it. "If anyone is demonstrating the need for solutions to the human side of our predicament, it is the 'hippies.' "[3]

It is this not caring that upsets the rest of the New Left, and, interestingly enough, the "straight" society as well, but for very different reasons. The hippie's unwillingness to recognize the interdependence of the entire social system, his unwillingness to accept the need to participate in a period of revolution, and his unwillingness to take part in the revolutionary generation all bother the rest of the New Left.

But the hippie's response is understandable. He is saying that he is creating the new life now. He is *living* the new life now. Why should he become involved in the revolution when he can have now what the revolution is for afterwards? This does not mean he does not care about the repression of contemporary society and the suffering of other people. He often meets with repression from the communities that surround his new commune. But he is saying that he is fighting here on his own ground to establish the life style that he wants. He is participating in the revolution by establishing alternative institutions that are like the institutions that would be expected to grow up after the revolution.[4]

But he is at least partially apolitical. One author characterized the hippies as emphasizing the following:[5]

Poverty
Exoticism—particularly Indian themes
Mysticism and withdrawal
Pastoral arcadianism
Togetherness

---

[3] Bowart and Katzman, "Sgt. Pepper's Political Club and Band," in Kornbluth (ed.), p. 197.

[4] Guy Strait, "What Is a Hippie?" *Maverick,* in ibid., pp. 201–3, in writing a response to "straight" society effectively answers the activists and revolutionaries, also, even though the details are different.

[5] Stuart Hall, "The Hippies: An American 'Moment'," in Julian Nagel (ed.), pp. 170–202.

Love
Here and now
Flower power
Higher perceptions—the inner life
Individualism: cultivating the self, doing your own thing

This list corresponds to a high degree to the various concepts that I have noted as being important to the New Left. The differences are more of degree than of kind. The emphasis on poverty, togetherness, love, higher perceptions, and individualism are all themes found in the rest of the New Left. The other themes— exoticism, mysticism, the arcadian life, and flower power—are not atypical of the New Left.

The hippie is stressing a combination of ideas concerned with transforming life today into the image of the future life held by most of the rest of the New Left. There are a few additions which emphasize gentleness, communion, and withdrawal.

The experience of the hippies in the Haight leads logically to a withdrawal from society and from activism. They were repressed both by contemporary society and its institutions and by those who presented themselves as being with them and of them. The experience of the Haight led the hippies to drop further out since it became impossible to trust even those who seemed to be like them. They found that many who presented themselves as hippies were only concerned with exploiting them. And they left the Haight to establish their lives in small communities in the country. Of course some left the Haight to become activists. Probably this was due to their experience there. But most of the hippies came to distrust those who did not live in their communities. The hippie started out as a gentle soul carrying flowers rather than knives and in some places where he has stayed in the city he now carries flowers *and* knives in order to protect himself from his friends and neighbors.[6]

The hippie alternative is one of the tactics of the New Left

---

[6] See Richard Goldstein, "Love: A Groovy Idea While He Lasted," *The Village Voice,* October 19, 1967, in Kornbluth (ed.), p. 258.

and it is one that should not be ignored by those looking at the activists and believing them to be the only tacticians. The split between hippie and activist is a very basic split within the New Left, but it arises partially because the two do not understand each other. Still, at the same time, in many cases it does represent very fundamental differences of opinion as to what an individual can and should do now with his life. The activist says that we must all be free together or none of us is free. The hippie says I am free now. The difference is important.

The reformers

When the Movement began with the civil rights movement in the South, the reformer dominated the Movement. Today the reformer is rare within the Movement. Still, even though he may be rare, and may shortly be nonexistent, he represents a position that has been important in the Movement and should be specified.

Logically a reformer can hold two separate positions. First, he can hold that the basic socio-political-economic system is good and that certain changes are needed in order to make it better. Secondly, he can hold that although the socio-political-economic system is bad, we are currently unable to change it completely, and therefore we should attempt to modify it as much as possible in order to ameliorate current conditions until it is possible to completely change the system. The civil rights movement started with the first position, but it would be inaccurate to say any longer that reformers of this sort belong to the New Left. There are a few reformers of the second sort who still remain.

Let us look very briefly then at the position of the second type of reformer and what it implies and the problems it raises. In a given situation in which one starts with the assumption that the socio-political-economic system is bad and must be radically transformed, one can take three positions. First, one may conclude that immediate revolution is possible and work for it. Second, one may conclude that immediate revolution is impossible, but that one should work to achieve it in order to bring it about more rapidly. Third, one can conclude that immediate revolution is impossible, and that one should work to change certain things within the system in order to improve contemporary conditions. A fourth position is conceivable of course—that immediate revolution is possible but that we should reform the system instead. With the basic assumption that the system is bad, however, the fourth position is contradictory so I shall ignore it.

The first two positions are those taken by revolutionaries; the third position is that taken by the reformers. This means that even though the system is bad, the conditions within the system are amenable to some change and improvement and change and improvement are valid and valuable in and of themselves. This is saying to the more radical or revolutionary position that one cannot forget the terrible conditions that causes them to say the system is bad during the period in which they are trying to overthrow the system. The reformer is saying to the revolutionary that we must work to change certain of the conditions that exist now at the same time as we attempt to overthrow the system. Stated in this last way, the distinction between the reformer and the activist is very thin. Most activists would also contend that it is desirable to try to ameliorate particular situations while attempting to work for the overthrow of the system. Therefore the distinction between reformers and activists may be more one of emphasis on reform versus emphasis on revolution than a difference in kind.

The reform position raises a peculiar problem that has been recognized by revolutionaries and debated at considerable length. Reform poses a dilemma for a revolutionary. On the one hand, if the revolutionary supports reform, and if the reform is successful in any small degree in ameliorating the conditions of contemporary society, it is likely that he has helped to put off the revolution. Time and time again a small improvement in living conditions directs people's attentions away from more radical solutions to the problems. Even though, as the revolutionary would contend, the problem itself was not solved but merely modified slightly, people tend to accept the temporary improvement and reject the more radical solution. On the other hand, if the revolutionary rejects reform in the name of a permanent solution through revolution, he is very likely to lose some of his support. He will lose support for precisely the same reason as he would lose support in working for successful reform. He will lose support because people are concerned most with their day-to-day affairs and possible improvements in those affairs. People are not concerned primarily with bringing about a radical transformation in their lives; most often they are concerned simply with improving their lives slightly. This may be why most revolutionaries come from middle-class conditions where most of the basic problems of existence have been solved adequately if not well, and people can then turn their attentions to broader questions of social conditions and the conditions of those not fortunate enough to be of the middle class.

The dilemma of reform is a very real one in the New Left today. There are objective conditions that need to be changed in the ghettos of the cities, in areas of rural poverty, in the treatment of women, and in the treatment of blacks and other minority groups. It is at least conceivable that some of these conditions can be improved through the system even if one still accepts the assumption that true solutions to the problems cannot be found within the system. But if conditions are bad enough to require a revolution, they must also be bad enough to require immediate reform and immediate improvement—unless the revolution is going to take place tomorrow. And even the most extreme professional revolutionary today does not expect the revolution to take place tomorrow or next week or even next year.

And thus the New Left is faced with the reform dilemma, and many of the activists are reformers in addition to being revolutionaries. One can only conclude that reform may put off the ultimate revolution, but that the New Left would seem to have no choice but to include reform within its activities.

The activists

Activists represent the largest and most important segment of the New Left. The contemporary activist is most likely to be a combination of a reformer and a revolutionary. Few activists yet think of themselves as professional revolutionaries, but more and more of them see revolution as the only solution to contemporary social problems.

Thus the activist is on the attack against contemporary institutions; he is aware of and looking for examples of repression; he is sensitive to the problems of contemporary society. The activist points out the problems and disabilities of contemporary society, and he is likely to participate in attempts to reform society at the local neighborhood or small-group level. He is particularly concerned with the establishment of alternative institutions within urban society that can replace contemporary institutions after the revolution.

The activist group is diverse. The best approach to understanding the diversity of tactical positions taken by activists will be to look at some examples of these positions.

Tom Hayden, for example, makes the following comments which illustrate one main position taken by activists:

"1. We must emphasize that the government is taking *political prisoners,* and reject the rulers' definition that we are 'law-breakers.' "

"2. We have to take care of our political prisoners."

"3. We need to expand our struggles to include a total attack on the courts."

"4. The people are the jury. We will win our particular cases as well as the general struggle . . . by taking the issues . . . to the public."

"5. We must become more international."

"6. We should stand on the right to self-defense and revolution. . . ."

"7. We must combine our separate movements into a united revolutionary front. . . ."[7]

Some of Hayden's points are widely disputed by people within the New Left, particularly point seven, but the general tenor of the argument is widely accepted.

---

[7] Tom Hayden, "Introduction," *Rebellion and Repression* (New York: Meridian Books, 1969), pp. 14–16. Emphasis in the original.

The first point emphasizes that activists consider themselves to be a suppressed minority very similar to surpressed minorities within other countries, such as the Soviet Union, where individuals are imprisoned for their political views. They believe that the American system is becoming more and more repressive of dissent. The New Left considers it quite reasonable to say that every person busted for possession of marijuana is a political prisoner. Marijuana often acts as a badge of separation of the new or counter-culture from the old culture, and one can see how this position can be accepted as reasonable by members of the New Left. Attacking the system symbolically by smoking marijuana does not automatically make one a member of the New Left, but the New Left sees the repression of this fairly mild form of dissent to be symbolic of repression by the system. Therefore there are thousands of political prisoners in American jails today.

The second argument that he makes is one of community or solidarity. He says that of the "thousands of people" in jail or facing trial today only a very few of them have the resources to adequately take care of themselves. The Movement then must insure them of support. In one sense the Movement sees all people who are in prison as being on their side. Anyone who attacks the system in any way can conceivably be seen as sympathetic to the New Left. Of course this is not in fact true. Many prisoners are as violently or more violently opposed to the New Left as those on the outside, but the point remains that the New Left can, with some slight justification, identify with any individual who has attacked the system in any way and thus been imprisoned.[8] And of course it can be more cogently argued that the legal, court, and jail system represent more clearly than anything else the repressive nature of contemporary society. Thus the identification with prisoners may be seen as an identification with those who have

---

[8] In *We Are Everywhere,* Jerry Rubin constantly reiterates the support the other prisoners had for the Chicago Seven while he was in jail.

faced the repression of the system, rather than a strict identification of interest.[9] This is carried out further by Hayden in the next
point, where he says that we must attack the court system and
demonstrate that it is not open and impartial in the way it is
presented but is actually "rigged."

Point four is of course the general notion of power to the people. Hayden is here contending that the concept of power to the
people is axiomatic for the New Left. He asserts, he does not
argue, that the best approach is to take both particular cases and
the whole struggle to the people rather than through the "rigged"
court system. He assumes that this is the only route for Movement
success.

Point five is a major concern of the New Left today. The Movement started in the United States in the civil rights movement
and later grew in the student and anti-war movements. At the
same time, movements among students were developing at various
other places around the world. Students in Europe, Asia, and
Latin America had been politically aware for much longer than
students in the United States, and their movements very rapidly
took on a more revolutionary stance than that in the United
States. The Movement in this country has begun to catch up with
the rest of the world, and it is attempting to develop an identity
and a unity with other movements around the world. In addition,
there is an explicit attempt, particularly by the Black Movement,
to identify and cooperate with Third World Movements in
Africa, Asia, and Latin America. The Black Movement sees itself
as a colony within the United States and thus can identify with
movements against colonial powers in other parts of the world.
"Black Power is not an isolated phenomenon. It is only another
manifestation of what is transpiring in Latin America, Asia, and
Africa."[10] Much of the New Left now sees itself as a colony

---

[9] See particularly Hayden, *Trial*.

[10] Lester, p. 138. See also Robert Blauner, "Internal Colonialism and
Ghetto Revolt," in Greer (ed.), originally published in the Spring 1969
issue of *Social Problems*.

within contemporary society and can thus also identify with movements around the world.[11]

But more importantly, the New Left and black movements identify with all attempts to attack capitalism, elite rule, and specifically the United States wherever and whenever they occur. Since capitalism and the United States are identified in the minds of many Americans and many people around the world, any attack on capitalism can be seen as an attack on the United States and as support for the positions of the New Left. Whether or not the support is explicit, the point remains the same. Any attack on the United States or capitalism or elite rule is interpreted on the New Left as helpful to the cause.

This point is best demonstrated by the fact that the major heros of the New Left are all anti-American revolutionists—Che, Mao, and Ho are the prime examples. Castro takes a back seat to Che in the list, but he is still a hero. And, lastly, Frantz Fanon, although he fought the French rather than the United States, was a revolutionary opponent of imperialism.

In his sixth point, Hayden argues for the right of self-defense and the right of revolution. This is an important theme on the New Left and the points he makes are interesting. He argues that the system will become more violent and more repressive as the Movement becomes more successful. There will be greater terror, there will be greater coercion, there will be greater repression and this will make for a more immediate revolution. The New Left should, although Hayden does not make this point explicitly, invite repression because repression breeds repression which breeds revolution. A revolutionary situation is produced by the repression of minority groups, and the more repression that exists, the more likely revolution becomes.

---

[11] See Barbara and John Ehrenreich, *Long March, Short Spring: The Student Uprising at Home and Abroad* (New York: Monthly Review Press, 1969); Nagel (ed.) op. cit.; and Joseph A. Califano, Jr., *The Student Revolution: A Global Confrontation* (New York: W. W. Norton & Co., 1970).

This is an important problem for the New Left. A full-scale attack on the New Left could probably still destroy it as a movement although it would drive many more into the ranks of the professional revolutionary and produce long-term sporadic internal conflict. But, on the other hand, *no* repression might destroy the New Left also. The Movement needs police overreaction. Chicago 1968 recruited more people to the New Left ranks than years of propaganda ever could.

Hayden's seventh point, that the separate movements within the United States must be combined, represents a major split within the Movement. The Black Movement and the Women's Movement do not accept this notion today. They argue that the New Left has been white-dominated and, in fact, racist- and male-dominated and, in fact, sexist. They are probably right. Therefore, even though people like Hayden want cooperation, the time for cooperation has passed, at least temporarily. The movements probably cannot be combined now or in the near future. Still, Hayden's point is important. The movements that exist in the United States today and in other countries do have many things in common that should, and perhaps can again, lead to significant cooperation and combination. If these movements can become united, they will provide a much greater force than has so far been seen.

Here it might be appropriate to look at a tactic which has so far proven to be what can only be called an abysmal failure, but which has exercised the New Left extensively and has proven to be very devisive. This is the student-worker alliance movement. Specific groups such as the Progressive Labor Party have focused on this particular approach, but it has had a significant attraction to a wide segment of the New Left. For a time in 1968 and continuing into 1970 and '71, it seemed as if the entire New Left was suddenly taken up with the idea of uniting the student or youth movement and workers.

Obviously the main reason for this attempt is related to the tradition of a workers or proletarian revolution.[12] It has been the assumption of most radical or revolutionary rhetoric since the early part of the 19th century that a worker or proletarian revolution was the only road to revolution, and in 1968 in Paris it seemed as if a student-worker alliance had in fact been formed and a revolution almost succeeded.

Revolutionary rhetoric still contends that the worker-student alliance formed in France in 1968 demonstrated the possibility of more widespread worker-student alliances, even though it is a matter of considerable dispute to what extent a real alliance was formed in 1968. On the one hand, there are the obvious cases of clear cooperation in demonstrations and in fighting with police. On the other hand, there are the Renault factory workers who locked out students who had come to support them. And finally, of course, the workers seemed to sell out the students for a little more money in their pay packets. But an attempt, which was at least partially successful, was made at that time. And even though it pointed up problems, and there were temporary splits, it has significant symbolic value to the New Left.

But whether student-worker alliances are possible within the conditions of the United States is a different question. On the one hand, there are student attempts to get to know workers, to take jobs in which they will be in daily contact with workers, and to "discuss politics with them."[13] These attempts have not been very successful. And, on the other hand, there are the "hard-hat" marches and demonstrations against the New Left.

But Hilary Putnam has suggested a more sophisticated approach, ". . . to build a student movement which consciously links

---

[12] See "Perspectives of the Left," in Jacobs and Landau, pp. 181–87. Originally published in the January 1969 issue of *Progressive Labor*.

[13] Fred Gordon, "Build the Campus Worker–Student Alliance," in John and Susan Erlich (eds.), *Student Power, Participation and Revolution* (New York: Association Press, 1970), p. 168. Originally published in the September 20, 1969, issue of *New Left Notes*.

up with the struggles of working people and the struggles of all oppressed people."[14] She then goes on to point out that a well-developed student movement, if it chooses the right issues, learns how to talk to workers, and fights its own antiworking-class attitudes, should be able to link up with workers to form an effective alliance.

Probably the only conditions in which this type of alliance can come about will be in a situation where the student leaves school and takes a job and gets to know the men and women with whom he or she works. But a student cannot appear to be primarily motivated by political considerations, for many of the workers will not understand him and will simply ignore him. Students who do not come out of a working-class background will have a difficult time learning the mores and standards of the people with whom they work because the mores and standards will be different from anything he or she will have previously experienced.

It is still considered important by parts of the New Left to develop a coalition between students and workers, particularly those parts that are tied most closely to the Old Left. It is still thought that no revolution can come about without participation by the workers. Although this may demonstrate the effects of accepting the ideology of the Old Left more than it demonstrates any careful and realistic analysis of contemporary society, it is still a significant issue for certain parts of New Left activism.

Probably the most positive tactic so far suggested by the New Left and attempted to be put into practice is the development of alternative institutions or alternative structures to the old society that can act both as a tactic of the struggle and an indication of the goal. Some of these alternative structures and institutions can be seen in such things as the popularity of the free school movement which takes education out of official buildings and puts them into people's homes and wherever education is possible, be it the

---

[14] Hilary Putnam, "From 'Resistance' to Student-Worker Alliance," in Long (ed.), p. 324.

street, the woods, or a library. The free school movement breaks down the traditional distance between teacher and student and establishes a situation in which all are considered to be both teachers and students, a situation which most teachers have always considered to be ideal. It also means that individuals do not have to go through rigidly prescribed curricula to the achievement of a degree whose characteristics have been established for centuries. It means that an individual studies what he or she wants, for whatever goals they perceive. This takes education out of a prescribed time period and extends it throughout one's entire life. The free school movement seems to be developing as a possibly significant alternative to our contemporary educational system.[15]

It can be seen as a significant goal in and of itself, but it should also be viewed as a tactic. The free school movement is a tactic in two senses. In one way it takes people out of the prescribed system with its rather limited and prescribed approach, and, it is to be hoped, allows individuals to explore their own interests. This is a part of the search for the authentic self and part of the process of freeing individuals from the contemporary system. Thus, in this first sense the free school system is an attempt to take individuals out of the control of contemporary society and allow them to develop within an alternative society. (Note also the similarity to the hippie position.)

It is also a tactic in that it points out many of the weaknesses of the contemporary educational system and acts as an attempt to reform or revolutionize that system. When the best students and the best teachers are beginning to leave the system or attack the fundamentals of the system, it has already been demonstrated that contemporary education is in need of great change.

---

[15] On the educational system, see Harold Taylor, *Students Without Teachers* (New York: McGraw-Hill, Inc., 1969); Staughton Lynd, "The Freedom Schools: Concept and Organization," in Teodori (ed.), pp. 102–5. Originally published in the April 1965, issue of *Freedomways*; and Ralph Keyes, "The Free Universities," in Jaffe and Tytell (eds.), pp. 177–89.

There are many ways in which other alternative institutions are being developed. For example, there are the attempts to remodel the basic family system. The family system has been modified in practice by the New Left in a variety of ways. It has been replaced by a totally communal system in which each member of the group is "married" to every other member of the group. In a very old, but growing, attack on the family system, many couples do not get married, but simply live together temporarily or permanently. Women are gaining greater equality within the family system by the establishment of communal child care and by the greater sharing of the work within the home among all members of the family, whether it be two people, a couple and their children, or a communal grouping. Thus the family system is being challenged directly as an institution by the establishment of significantly modified family structures.

The whole communal movement is an attempt to develop an alternative institution, or perhaps it would be more accurate to say an entire alternative society. The communal system is an attempt to establish new living patterns, new life styles, new settlement patterns, and new work patterns. Thus the communal movement is a direct challenge to the basic structure of society and a direct attempt to establish an alternative.

There are many more alternative institutions being developed, ranging from alternative news media, alternative film groups and movie houses, alternative magazines, to alternative religions, alternative political systems within neighborhoods, and alternative life styles. Development of alternative institutions by the New Left is one of the most significant of its tactics. It sees itself as building the new society now and providing its members with an opportunity to leave completely the old society. Even for those who do not join alternative societies or communes, there are significant alternative institutions available for them so that they do not have to participate as extensively in the old society.

There are still other tactics, from "ripping off" (shoplifting or any form of stealing from the system) to revolution. The practice of ripping off stores is considered by many to be a true attack on the system. In this way, one causes the store a great deal of trouble and costs them money. In addition, the individual is able to provide himself with needed goods, clothing, and so forth without having to earn the money to buy them. Ripping off causes a fair amount of debate in some groups and there are certain limitations assumed. It is generally assumed that one will only steal from large organizations, and that one will not attack individuals directly through stealing from the individually-owned store. Still, many see ripping off as simply passing the cost onto others who may or may not be able to afford it, since the stores simply mark up the prices of their goods to cover the stolen goods. But it is fair to say that many activists today feel that ripping off is an acceptable tactic.

There are many other of these individual tactics that are used against the system, but most of them have been used by unions in the past in demands for higher wages, such as a little sand in the gears by accident or a high rate of poor quality material being produced. Others came out of the civil rights, student, and anti-war movements and should be looked at briefly.

The protest or demonstration that came most directly out of the early movement was originally considered to be purely nonviolent. Particularly in the civil rights movement in the South, individuals were expected to respond non-violently to all violence, and one of the early youth movements, SNCC, was named the Student Non-Violent Coordinating Committee. It was originally nonviolent, but then, while still calling itself SNCC, the members concluded that if they were to be treated violently, there was no reason why they should not be able to respond with violence.[16]

The tendency in demonstrations has been to move from nonviolent, peaceful sit-downs and sit-ins to more active stone throwing, building burnings, and bombings. But the central focus has

---

[16] There are a number of works listed in the bibliography that trace out this development.

still been on protest with voice and body against an institution or an individual that represents a repressive society. This has been seen most often in connection with universities. Schools have been shut down on strikes or protests against activities that were either directly or very indirectly related to the educational system. But the argument is quite simple—the school is part of the repressive system, so that attacking any part is like attacking any other part.[17] The demonstration or protest has been a significant part of the tactics of the New Left and participation in protests, time in jail, scars from the police, and lungs seared with tear gas or eyes burned with mace are badges of the Movement. An individual who participates in a protest, whether peaceful or not so peaceful, finds some sense of community and solidarity with his fellows; he may find what for him is a valid approach to changing society and thus learn much about his true self; and most importantly he directly experiences the repressive nature of the response.

American youth were shocked by the shootings at Kent State.[18] They had not really expected that the repressive system would kill its own children. Kent State led to two phenomena on the New Left—an escalation of violence, and a greater dropping out because the society was simply not worth the attempt to save it.

Protest and demonstration of greater and greater violence has been seen by the media to be the major tactic of the New Left, but even for the activists, although the results of the demonstrations are badges of the revolution, the protest has not been the major part of the attack. The attack has been based upon alternative institutions, demonstrations of the repressive nature of the system, and a whole variety of attempts to attack the system, including the protest. But it is simply too limiting to focus on the protest as the most important activity. It is one of many activist activities.

---

[17] See, for example, North American Congress on Latin America, "Who Rules Columbia?" Teodori (ed.), pp. 335–45.

[18] See Ottavio M. Casale and Louis Paskoff (eds.), *The Kent Affair, Documents and Interpretation* (Boston: Houghton Mifflin Co., 1971).

Professional revolutionaries

"Tonight, at 7 p.m., we blew up the NYC Police headquarters."[19] Perhaps for the first time since the American Revolution, there has developed within American society a group of dedicated professional revolutionaries who see the tactics of the bomb as a major part of their attack on the system. Since Weatherman and the Black Panthers are the major, if not the only representatives of the professional revolutionary in the New Left, I shall look at the ideas of these groups. Weatherman was founded in 1969 in the major split of the SDS into the Progressive Labor and Revolutionary Youth Movement factions. Then in the same year Weatherman split off from the Revolutionary Youth Movement to form a movement of their own. Later, in 1970, Weatherman went underground to form a group dedicated to the violent overthrow of the government. Weatherman has claimed credit for a series of bombings and for the escape of Timothy Leary from prison.[20] (It is noteworthy that the prisons of the country are now considered to be prisoner of war camps by groups such as Weatherman.) The basic doctrine of Weatherman as expressed in a variety of its writings, appears on the surface to be similar to the revolutionary positions of the Third World. The focus is on imperialism and on the colonial status of the Blacks. Weatherman holds that it is part of a revolutionary working class vanguard for the elimination of U.S. imperialism and colonialism within the United States.[21] They are strongly anticapitalist, as is the entire New Left, and it must be said that they are heros to the rest of the New Left even when it does not emulate them. Weather-

---

[19] "Communique #2 from the Weatherman Underground," in Jacobs (ed.), p. 512.

[20] See "Communique #4 from the Weatherman Underground" and "Letter from Timothy Leary" in Jacobs (ed.), pp. 516–19.

[21] See "You Don't Need a Weatherman to Know Which Way the Wind Blows" in Jacobs (ed.), pp. 51–90.

man members who were killed in the accidental explosion of a bomb in a New York City apartment have been eulogized in poem and song.[22] Together with the four at Kent State, many of the members of the Black Panthers who have died in battles with the police,[23] Che Guevara, Ho Chi Minh, and Mao Tsetung, they make up the panoply of heros and martyrs of the Movement today.

The question of tactics involved in Weatherman activities is fairly simple. The U.S. system of imperialism and capitalism has become so intolerable that it must be immediately destroyed. Reform, protest, and alternative institutions are fine in their place, but it is too late for them. Weatherman believes that only through immediate attacks on the system can meaningful change be brought about.

Racism, imperialism, and male chauvanism are so deeply ingrained in the repressive institutions of contemporary society that they are incapable of reformation. Thus any attack on any institution, any building, or any person, is permissible and desirable. The Weathermen have not yet attacked individuals directly but they have glorified people like Charles Manson[24] for the murders he and his clan committed. Weatherman views violence of almost any sort as desirable.

They are self-consciously a guerilla army within the United States, modeled on the guerilla forces of Castro in Cuba, Che in Bolivia, and the Viet Cong, although Weatherman glorifies violence much more than these guerillas do. Direct action guerilla warfare is a new phenomenon in this country, but it represents

---

[22] See "In Memory of Ted Gold," "For Diana Oughton," "For Terry Robbins," and "How Does It Feel to be Inside an Explosion . . ." in Jacobs (ed.), pp. 484, 481–90, and 504–8.

[23] There are some who believe that such deaths have been much overstated. See Edward Jay Epstein, "Reporter at Large; C. R. Garry's List of Panthers Allegedly Killed by Police, With Case Histories," *The New Yorker*, Vol. 46 (February 13, 1971), pp. 45–46+. Comment: Vol. 47 (May 8, 1971), p. 125.

[24] See "Stormy Weather" in Jacobs (ed.), p. 347.

both the frustration of growing segments of the New Left and the symbols of struggle around the world. Weatherman identifies with the Black Panthers, the Arab guerillas, the Viet Cong, the Chinese peasant of the Chinese Revolution, Castro's revolutionary movement, and all other guerilla movements around the world that are directed at U.S. imperialism.

The only other group in the United States that tends in this direction is the Black Panthers. Although they are usually blamed for all acts of violence against the system that take place in American ghettos, it has seldom been demonstrated that they are in fact to blame. The Black Panthers do argue that political power comes out of the mouth of a gun, as did Mao Tse-tung, but they have found that on the whole if a black man carries a gun in this country he doesn't need to use it. Simply carrying it frightens the white American sufficiently.

Most guerilla warfare has been focused on rural areas and capturing and maintaining control of the countryside. The position of the urban guerilla is unusual in the context of guerilla warfare and has not been adequately defined. The Weathermen are the prototypical urban guerilla.

The beginning of the revolution in an urban situation is a period of harassment. It is a time during which the guerilla forces, the professional revolutionaries, attack widely dispersed points in cities around a country with bombings and disruptions of everyday activities. The guerilla is a full-time revolutionary attacking points with a variety of tactics, not always with bombs, but with whatever weapons are at hand. Mobility, speed, careful preparation, great courage and dedication, and an ability to blend into the surroundings and disappear are the essential characteristics of an urban guerilla.

Mao specifies in the tenth point of his military tactics for guerilla warfare[25] that a territorial base is required which is vir-

---

[25] Mao Tse-tung, *Selected Works* (Peking: Foreign Language Press, 1961), Vol. 4, p. 162.

tually free from attack, where a guerilla is able to rest and train for future actions. This territorial base is even more important to an urban guerilla than it is to a rural guerilla. The urban guerilla must be able to disappear very rapidly into his surroundings because of the overwhelmingly superior force against him. The Weathermen have found that they can disappear very easily into the youth ghettos around the country. The Black Panthers can very easily disappear into the black ghettos around the country. It is easy to move from city to city on the highways either thumbing or driving. It is easy to both blend in and move around. This is the greatest tactic of the urban guerilla: the ability to disappear in one city and appear in another city. "For you to survive must mean that thousands of kids everywhere are enough like you that the pigs can't isolate you to pick you off."[26]

"Today we attack with rocks, riots and bombs the greatest killer-pig ever known to man—Amerikan imperialism."[27] This statement found in "Communique Number Three from the Weatherman Underground" is indicative of the position of the Weatherman today. We must, they say, attack American imperialism wherever and whenever it is found, with whatever means are at hand. The Weathermen are self-consciously the vanguard of the revolution. They are accepted as the violent vanguard by many people of the New Left today. Many on the New Left today are very disillusioned with the possibility of significant change and Weatherman seems to some to be trying to do something about it.

The violence of Weatherman has not had a great appeal on the New Left in the past. On the one hand, the New Left is becoming more violent, more dedicated to the violent overthrow of the system, less concerned with how this overthrow is accomplished, but, on the other, there is a mood of inward looking that is affecting many of the New Left today. This is not to imply that the Movement has slowed down or has significantly changed.

---

26 "Notes to the Underground" in Jacobs (ed.), p. 513.

27 "Communique #3 from the Weatherman Underground" in Jacobs (ed.), p. 515.

It will arise again in response to some clear action of repression, or it will arise again spontaneously in an attack on the system. In the meantime, Weatherman, the Black Panthers, and others of their type are keeping the Movement alive in the direction of violence.

In addition, the Women's groups and various activists are keeping the Movement very much alive in the lives of each individual active in these groups, and there are thousands of them. The New Left has quieted down now to reconsider its tactics, to reconsider its position, and to look at itself with a view to coming out again and changing the system and the lives of each individual within the system.

Many youths leave the system each day. They drop out into activism or they drop out into rural communes. But the important point may be not that they take one form of rejection of the system or another form, but that they reject the system.

8

CONCLUSION

Having looked at the New Left in some detail, and having noted some of the interrelationships among the ideas of the New Left, it only remains to summarize the basic concepts and to specify more clearly the interrelationships that hold among the basic ideas.

I shall do this in two ways. First, I shall look at the New Left vision of the future society as a whole. Then I shall summarize the specific values of the New Left, discussing the hierarchy of values and the relationships among them. Finally, by way of conclusion, I shall look at the New Left in perspective to see if it can be placed in the development of radical thought.

The New Left utopia

To present the New Left picture of its utopia or their vision of the future society, I will first break up that complex of interactions that we call society into its constituent units. All societies have the following:

1. A political system.
2. An economic system.
3. A socialization system.
4. A social stratification and mobility system.[1]

---

[1] The New Left, of course, rejects the notion that this system is necessary.

By presenting the vision of future society along these lines, recognizing the divisions purely for descriptive purposes, it is possible to gain a picture of the New Left utopia.

The best place to start is the setting. Earlier I indicated that the New Left vision of the far future was one in which urban centers had been broken up and replaced with small communities. This provided a physical setting of small towns surrounded by fields. Each town could be a work of art in itself, with the buildings designed for human rather than machine purposes, and to establish a sense of community. This vision of the far future gives us one of the possible settings for the New Left utopia, only one of a number of possibilities suggested by New Left thought, of course, but the most consistent with the premises.

Another setting can be seen in what may best be called a period of transition from where we are now to that vision of the far future. The urban centers still remain but have been improved and cleaned up and some of the congestion broken up by the establishment of some small communities. In his novel *The Napoleon of Notting Hill* (1904), G. K. Chesterton presented a picture of London broken up into the traditional neighborhood groupings that had grown together to form the city. Although Chesterton is ambivalent about the value of the society he presents, the basic idea is not significantly different from the notion of the New Left of breaking up urban areas into small neighborhood communities.

Thus the physical setting for this transitional period would be characterized by a series of neighborhoods, perhaps surrounded by park land or even not identifiably cut off from other neighborhoods, but with an inward looking character rather than a broad urban or metropolitan character. This may seem to go against the general internationalism and cosmopolitanism of the New Left, but the stress on the small community implies this return to the inward looking town.

The work situation will have been diversified so that individuals can work in or close to their communities rather than traveling one or more hours each day. The focus of life is on the neighborhood, not split between the living situation and the work situation. There are no "bedroom" communities. Even in this transitional period, and even if it does not move beyond that, the focus is changed to one of neighborhood units.

In this picture of the physical setting there is one of the keys to the whole New Left vision—diversity. One of the most basic ideas of New Left thought is a deep concern with and emphasis on the individual human being in all of his complexity. There is no notion here of a basic unchangeable or unchanging human nature, but there is a fundamental idea that individuals are diverse and should be capable of finding living situations within which that diversity is accepted and actively encouraged. Therefore the basic settlement pattern is one in which neighborhoods or small communities encourage individuals to try differing life styles in differing locations. Even the political system, which is usually seen as a force for integrating or pulling together the diverse elements of a community, emphasizes diversity.

To some extent the political system still fulfills this major function for the New Left. The New Left does not see society as a mere combination of discrete individuals but as a community of individually unique people. The system must be looked at first from its lowest level, the small community. Here there are only enough people so that they can get to know each other and deal with each other individually or personally on a day-to-day basis. Also, they are likely to be in similar work situations so that their work interests are bound together.

Therefore, there is a situation in which individuals have common interests. They live close to each other. They know each other. And they have ties of friendship and even love. These people meet whenever one or more of them feels the need. The meetings could be called fairly simply due to the smallness of the group involved and would probably come about simply through the process of discussion of a problem that is suggested by one of the group. The discussion would continue informally until it seemed that a meeting was called for. At that point a meeting could be called by anyone in the group.

In this meeting there would probably be no formal procedures, although there would be some sort of recording secretary who would attempt to summarize the discussion at appropriate points. This recording secretary would be chosen at each meeting either by random selection through lot, or rotation, or by someone volunteering. The meeting would proceed essentially on the lines of the previous pre-meeting discussion: Individuals would present their ideas on the particular issue as they felt moved to do so. Those who had no particular concern with the issue would either not attend the meeting or would not become intimately involved in it. Those who were concerned with the issue would try, through the process of presentation, clarification, and discussion of positions, to reach a mutually agreeable conclusion. The process of discussion at the meeting would continue not until some vote at the close of the meeting but until the discussion reached a mutually agreeable conclusion. If such a conclusion were not reached in the first meeting, other meetings would be held. The assumption is that these are people who are willing and able to work out an agreement that is acceptable to the whole community, and that they are not on an "ego trip" which keeps them from seeing other positions and other possibilities.

This first level should be sufficient for most of the day-to-day affairs of the community. For intercommunal problems, a similar process would take place. Either through mutual recognition of and consultation over a common problem or by one group suggesting to another group that a common problem existed, a process very like the one just described would take place. The question would be discussed informally within each community. A meeting or meetings within the community might be held. An individual or a small group would be chosen, on any number of bases, to act for the community in more detailed discussions with an agent or agents of the other community. These individuals would be given a wide variety of types of instructions from a fairly free hand to very specific or detailed instructions. And they would be bound to report back to the community regularly.

The assumption is that relationships among the communities would proceed upon a basis of mutual trust rather than mutual antagonism. With this assumption operative, the cooperation among communities could function approximately as well as the cooperation within the communities. Laws would not be passed, but community decisions would be made by and for everyone in the community, and an individual's unwillingness to accept the decision should normally cause the community to reconsider the decision. Intercommunal agreements would not be reached without the same sort of participation by each individual, only slightly less directly. Laws would not be enforced by the community; individuals would willingly accept the way a community functioned, or they could participate directly in changing the procedures. And with many small communities the individual would have the option of sampling different life styles and finding ones that most suited his own personality.

Disputes should be rare. Individuals with disagreements should in most cases be able to work them out among themselves. Those disputes that had to be referred to the community as a whole would be treated in the same way as any other decision—everyone would participate. In all these ways the political system is based upon direct participation and consensual agreement.

It should be obvious that these procedures require people to be willing to cooperate actively and participate actively without rancor. The system would probably fail to work if people are unwilling to accept decisions that are not exactly what they want. Everyone must be willing to adjust to the needs and desires of others while still supporting his/her own beliefs.

The economic system would reflect some of the changes that have already been noted. First, it would be decentralized. Large industrial complexes would be broken up into small industries. Efficiency would not be the primary value. The human being would be the primary value, and would not be seen as an extension of a machine but as the main reason for the operation of the system. Human needs would be primary; machine needs would be secondary. Thus with a decentralized economic system focusing on the needs and desires of the people in each community, the economic system should be significantly humanized.

Each community would produce as much as possible for itself. Its members would produce their own food to the extent possible. This means, first, that many of the exotic items that we have come to expect as a normal part of our diet would probably no longer be available, since the concern would be with self-sufficiency. Once that point were reached, trade for more exotic items would most likely take place, but—with the emphasis on reducing need—such luxuries would not be encouraged. The diet would depend, in part at least, upon where the community was located, but of course some trade would be essential. Thus there will always have to be some intercommunity cooperation. No community (or at least very few) can be totally self-sufficient agriculturally.

Of course, each community would not be purely agricultural. Each community would include some small industry and some craft industries. The New Left emphasizes the redevelopment of hand work as a particularly creative outlet for the individual. Thus it is to be expected that each community would develop some craftsmen who would produce both for the community and for limited trade outside of the community.

Before all this could take place, there would be a long period of transition. Each community in this period would produce what it could for itself, but it would be limited by its location, perhaps within an urban area, and would thus specialize in a particular good or service that could be traded to other communities in exchange for food and other necessary goods and services. General goals and plans would be established by the community, and the specific work situation would be controlled by the workers.

One very important part of the economic system, and a part that is essential to understanding it, is the rejection of materialism and consumerism. The economic system would not be designed to produce more and more unnecessary items, but for the production of a limited number of high-quality goods. Individuals would not be expected to collect household items that primarily reflect status rather than being of any real value. An individual would have fewer things, but they would be better, and they would be a more direct reflection of his or her personality. Each individual would reduce his wants so that everyone in the community would be well provided for in quality of food, housing, and life in general. "Well" does not mean "well" in contemporary terms of many goods, conspicuous consumption, and extravagant living, but it does not mean poverty, either. It would mean for all a degree of comfort that relatively few people reach today because it would reflect each individual's needs and desires. Each individual would be free to express himself rather than feeling bound by convention.

This society would be leisure-based and would use whatever automation and other labor-saving devices available, particularly in the industrial work situation. The economic system would play a smaller role in the future society than it does today. It would be community controlled; the work situation would be controlled by the workers. There would be fewer goods produced, but at the same time, each individual would be better able to express himself in his possessions than he is today.

The socialization system is, most simply, the means by which a society passes on its major goals and values to the next generation. In talking about this system it is customary to focus on such institutions as the family, the church, the educational system, and the mass media. In the New Left utopia, each of these institutions would be radically transformed. Each would emphasize the free development of free and loving individuals rather than competitive, work-oriented individuals.

The family system would probably be the most radically transformed of all the aspects of society. At the same time it is possible that the nuclear family system of parents and children would be maintained by some communities—but even where it is, it is likely to be modified. For example, in Aldous Huxley's novel *Island* (1962), the suggestion is made that children be brought up by a variety of people in the neighborhood, changing the living conditions as the children or the parents and neighbors wish. This suggestion has recently been picked up and looked at seriously (or re-created by somebody else) by those concerned with maintaining the nuclear family system while producing a better situation for raising children.

Another contemporary change that could be part of either the nuclear family system or some other modified sort of family is the rapid development of day-care centers. This is very important to the New Left since such centers are concerned with procedures for freeing the woman, or both parents, from the total responsibility for their children. If a person must spend most of her/his time for a large segment of their lives caring for her/his children, she/he is likely to be limited significantly in the ability to develop her/his own interests and personality. The day-care center is an important but small reform to bring about the freeing of individuals to develop themselves. If this reform is significantly expanded, it could have far-reaching effects, and the New Left sees it both as something that can be done now to free people and as part of a modified family system in the future.

Turning to more complete changes in the family system, here is a list of a few alternatives. Each can be found now in society and would be found, encouraged, and developed in the future society.

1. Group marriage in which each individual has sexual relations with all other individuals and the children are raised by the group.
2. Couples living together for long or short periods with or without children.
3. Communes which are based on the nuclear family with children communally raised.
4. Gay communes.

Though each of these systems can be found today, most of them are not accepted by society in general. In the future these diverse life styles would be generally accepted and encouraged.

It is very difficult to say from a current picture of the New Left what religion might look like in the future. There is a religious upsurge among the drop-out segment but it is so diverse that it is hard to generalize about it. The only safe generalization seems to be that religion will still exist, and it will be as diverse as it is today. Perhaps the chief differences will be found in the acceptance and encouragement of this diversity and specifically in the acceptance and encouragement of atheism.

The educational system as we know it today will disappear. An educational system designed for free, loving individuals will have no need of rigid classrooms, rigid hours, rote learning, and competition. Children will be taught the basic skills in their communities by other children and by the adults in the community. The job will not be assigned to one person but will be considered a community responsibility. Children will search out individuals with interests that they want to develop. We know that a child who develops an interest in something can bring a phenomenal learning energy to it. This will be encouraged, rather than discouraged as it often is today. The child will be expected to experiment and will be encouraged to look into a variety of aspects of knowledge and styles of life. The child as he or she matures will be expected to spend considerable time in exploring different life styles in different communities rather than being molded into the life style of the community in which he is brought up. Diversity will be encouraged. There will be few school buildings. Everyone will be a teacher and everyone will be a student.

Since the society is not concerned with producing people to produce and consume, the school will be able to take individual differences into account. The individual will be encouraged to develop his own interests rather than those that are currently of interest to the society. A free and loving community will accept and encourage its children to find themselves rather than to fit a mold.

The mass media will be community-run and diversity will be

encouraged. The large daily newspaper will disappear in favor of a variety of small news sheets, pamphlets, and books. Everyone will have access to the media. But since people will live in face-to-face situations in which they know the life of the community, there will be much less need for the news media. Programs of entertainment will be primarily community-developed. There will be community theater, community-produced movies, and community television. Generally the media will be communal and diverse and each individual will have access to them.

As I noted earlier, the New Left does not accept social stratification as necessary. This does not mean that everyone will be the same or that social groupings will not exist. It means that invidious distinctions among people will disappear. Therefore there will be no clear social mobility system either. The only thing at all comparable to today will be the ability of an individual to move freely from community to community, sampling different life styles.

The value system

In the foregoing I have suggested some of the basic values of the New Left, such as diversity and community, and I have looked at others throughout the book. In this section what is needed is a brief summary of these values so that it will be possible to see how they relate to each other and specifically which ones are the most important.

The first chapter of this book, "The Search For the Authentic Self," points out a number of the basic values of the New Left. First, there is individuality, the focus on and emphasis on the individual as a discrete, unique entity, an entity that must be encouraged to develop a sense of self and a sense of personal value. Secondly, there is a concern with diversity as it links to individuality. Each individual, in being unique, provides society with the basis for great variety. This individuality and diversity provides the third of the values of the New Left, freedom. I looked specifically at freedom in the chapter titled "Do Your Own Thing," where I noted that the New Left conception of freedom was first based upon this notion of individuality and that it would be a main value of the future society in and of itself. Freedom to express individuality and a variety of unique individuals is a basic value to the New Left. All of these values can be seen as coming directly out of the notion of the search for the authentic self, and each is directly related to the basic problem of the search, the ability to overcome alienation.

This ability, I then noted, depended on another major value, community, as well as the values already mentioned. This major value of community I defined as a society organized on the basis of close or intimate interpersonal relationships within a small geographical area which encouraged diversity and individuality. Community can be seen as an adjunct to the search for the authentic self or as a separate value which the New Left stresses in and of itself because of its rejection of contemporary society in which each individual is isolated from every other individual and from himself. I noted that the New Left argued that only within a community would individuals be able to overcome alienation from themselves and from others. I also noted that it was only within a community work situation that an individual would be able to overcome the alienation from work that is the third major aspect of alienation. Thus, community is a basic goal and a major value for the New Left.

Finally, I pointed out that the notion of equality was historically the first and most important value of the New Left, and that it had remained as a significant aspect of New Left thought. But I said that it had remained so because of its historical importance and because of its importance to two major segments of the Movement today, black radicalism and the Women's Liberation Movement. And I said that it remained because of the basic argument that only within a system of equality would it be possible for the individual to function within a community, find his authentic self, and overcome alienation. Thus, equality is in part a goal in opposition to contemporary society and in part a specific mechanism within the future society for making that future society work. In the latter case, equality can be seen to fulfill a secondary but very significant role in relation to the idea of community.

These, then, are the main goals and values of the New Left. It should be clear that they are intimately entwined. One of the most important points that must be made about the New Left is that it holds an identifiable complex of ideas that are all related to one another. Although individuals and groups within the Movement may disagree over emphases and tactics, the basic values and goals are the same.

For two reasons it is very difficult to specify precisely the hierarchy of values. First, it is always difficult to be certain what is intended by any group unless they specify clearly their hierarchy of values, and the New Left has not done this. Second, the New Left is particularly concerned that forms should be worked out in specific situations rather than that general values be established. I have been able to say that the New Left utopia or vision of the future would take fairly specific forms, but in doing so I did not have to extrapolate very far from current procedures and practices and ideals and goals as they have been stated by the New Left. In discussing the values of the New Left throughout this book I did not have to fill in very much that was left out or go into areas that had not been covered by contemporary New Left thought. When I talk about the hierarchy of values, however, I come to an unclear area. Therefore the following statements should be taken as very tentative.

The two values that are the most important are unfortunately potentially conflictual. These are community, on the one hand, and the individuality-diversity-freedom complex, on the other. It cannot be said which of these two values takes first place in the hierarchy. The New Left sees them as inseparable. They do not see a way of dividing the community situation from an emphasis on individuality and freedom. The community system is designed to allow for the development of individuality, diversity, and freedom. Still, there is a problem: What happens if there is a conflict between individual freedom and communal desires? I showed how this worked out in the political realm a little earlier. In that discussion individuality and freedom were primary because I said that the community would be likely to reconsider a problem about which there was conflict. But at the same time I emphasized that conflict would be highly unlikely for exactly the reasons of community life, communion, friendship, love, and security—thus illustrating the point the New Left is making about these two values: both are equal. Only in a specific situation would it be possible for a specific group of people to work out their own hierarchy of values and choose, if it were necessary to do so, between freedom and individuality, on the one hand, and community, on the other.

As I noted in talking about the concept of equality, it is a secondary concept tied to the others. Within contemporary society it is seen as a primary goal because of the obvious inequalities of the system and their bad effects. As a value, though, equality is tied to the notions of community and individuality because it is assumed that only in a community in which basic equalities of treatment exist can individual freedom be truly meaningful for everyone.

Closely tied to the idea of equality is the notion that our life has been too concerned with the material and that we should reduce our wants in order to begin to find ourselves. The reduction of consumerism with its emphasis on material goods relates to an entire range of changes in life style and social system from a society and culture based upon work to one based upon leisure. In addition, there would be a change in the work situation to one that is part of community life. The change of life situation is intimately tied with the values of equality and community and freedom. It is tied to equality in the sense that some economic equality will be brought about by reducing need and thus the goods produced will be able to be distributed more evenly. It is linked to the notion of community in that the work situation will be part of community life rather than separate from it. It is linked, most importantly, to freedom and individuality because it means that by reducing our material possessions we will be able to come closer to finding ourselves, and it means that with the changed need structure we will be able to free ourselves from the present, alienated work situation to an unalienated work situation that is just one part of a complex of activities in which we are expressing our authentic selves.

The New Left in perspective

I have pointed out that the New Left basically agrees with the major goals and values that have been held by Western civilization for centuries—self-fulfillment, liberty, equality, and community. At the same time, the New Left stresses the need for revolutionary change and the need to do away with all or almost all government. Its stress on revolution and the abolition of government puts the New Left among the more radical political philosophies. Finally, its attitudes toward such social institutions as the family and the educational system again separates it significantly from much of the value system that is generally associated with contemporary Western culture. Since none of the positions taken by the New Left is unique, it will be worthwhile to attempt to place the New Left in some overall perspective and particularly to note its affinities with other aspects of radical thought.

The New Left seems to develop out of two of the major streams of radicalism—Marxian socialism and anarchism. The first of these, Marxian socialism, the New Left uses for its criticism of contemporary society and for many of its specific revolutionary heroes. The second, anarchism, the New Left draws upon for many of its major goals. This is not to say in either case that the similarities are consciously or intentionally established by the New Left, but the similarities do exist. There are obviously a number of other traditions that could be linked to the New Left, particularly Romanticism and the whole "return to the land" approach, but while these traditions impinge on the New Left and other parts of radical thought, the New Left clearly identifies and can be most identified with the two streams of thought first noted here. (It would not be of much help to point out all the other possible currents of thought that the New Left can be related to because the relationship, while existing, is not yet demonstrably significant.)

The critique of contemporary society given by the New Left stems in large part from its perception of the bad effects of capitalism and competition. The effects I have noted are:

1. Alienation from self.
2. Alienation from others—lack of community.
3. Alienation from work—man, the extension of the machine.
4. Lack of freedom.
5. Inequality—destruction of the chances of many for the benefit of a few.

These, plus many other problems (such as pollution) are believed to stem from capitalism and competition. A number of these points were made by Marx, and later Marxists have made them more explicitly applicable to contemporary society.[2]

The argument goes somewhat as follows. The competitive capitalistic society produces all of these evils as a result of its basic class nature and because of the internal characteristics of capitalism which require greater and greater production of goods, exploitation of workers, exploitation of underdeveloped nations, and elite rule. All of these points are part of the New Left critique in specifically Marxist terms. The New Left has still managed to stay away from some of the dogmatisms of the Old Left, although it is developing some of its own, and the New Left tends to put the critique in terms that are more understandable and relevant to contemporary readers than the Old Left's.

Specifically, although some of the New Left note the basic

---

[2] There is a vast Marxist literature on this, so it is only possible to suggest a few important examples. See Baran and Sweezy; Leszek Kolakowski, *Towards a Marxist Humanism: Essays on the Left Today;* trans. Jane Zielonko Peel (New York: Grove Press, Inc., 1968); and Adam Schaff, *Marxism and the Human Individual,* trans. Olgierd Wojtasiewicz, Robert S. Cohen, ed. (New York: McGraw-Hill Book Co., 1970).

class nature of contemporary society, the New Left is more likely to put the critique in terms of inequality rather than in terms of economic class. Thus, although some of the New Left sees the black as equivalent to the degraded proletariat of Marxist analysis, most on the New Left do not put it in such terms. Instead, the position of the black is discussed in more general terms, such as the need for the system to maintain a pool of unskilled labor to draw upon in times of rapid economic expansion—"an acceptable level of unemployment." Racism is seen as a necessary part of this exploitation of the black because the exploitation would not be accepted by the black or the rest of society without the assumption of actual physical or biological difference that racism gives.

The same explanation is given for sexism. The capitalist system requires a pool of unskilled to semiskilled laborers to handle the paper work and the other uninteresting or dull tasks of the day-to-day routine. Since men do not provide a sufficient supply of this, women are used. In addition, the man in a competitive situation needs someone to look down upon at all times; thus, the position of women. Third, the system requires a large amount of worthless produce to be consumed and the status of women makes them the ideal consumer. Fourth, and this is an explicit part of the Marxian analysis, the woman is a part of the man's property held in bondage to insure that his property is passed on to his progeny at his death. Fifth, the woman is a status symbol—the less she has to do, the more status she gives the man.

Hence the New Left critique of both racism and sexism draws upon the Marxian tradition, but it can be said that the New Left analysis is more appropriate for contemporary conditions. The major inequalities in society are believed to be a direct result of the needs of the capitalist system. The logic of the situation is therefore obvious: In order to get rid of these inequalities, a desirable goal, the capitalist system must be destroyed.

I have noted earlier the way in which the New Left has taken the notion of alienation from Marx and applied it. Marx talked about alienation in three ways: from self, from others, and from work. The New Left applies all of these to contemporary society. Both Marx and the New Left see the reasons for this alienation as stemming primarily from capitalism. The work situation is obvious: Man is an extension of the machine as a direct result of the need of the capitalist system to produce more and more goods. The division from others is also obvious: Competition cannot help but divide man from man. The alienation from self is slightly less obvious, but can be looked at it in two ways. First, the alienation from others and from work will produce alienation from self. Second, the capitalist system forces an individual into a mold or a way of life that never allows him to discover his true self and his real interests. The capitalist system sees the individual as a producer and a consumer. These are the only two routes within which an individual is allowed to fulfill himself and the individual is trained to believe that this is good and true. Therefore again the Marxian analysis and the New Left critique of contemporary society are similar. They both note in the same way that the capitalist system produces alienation.

It should be clear from the foregoing that the New Left is convinced that in such conditions as today's, freedom, true freedom, is impossible. True freedom can only come after alienation has been overcome and alienation cannot be overcome in a capitalist situation. In addition true freedom is based on the ability of an individual to do "his own thing" or to find himself. Since he is trained to be a producer and consumer, it is impossible for him to find himself. Therefore, the basis for true freedom does not and cannot exist under capitalism. Finally, in a society based on standardization, diversity is considered undesirable. The contemporary capitalist system accepts standardization and while the occasional eccentric is permitted, large masses of eccentrics are not unless they can be kept within the producing-consuming framework. Diversity and eccentricity are acceptable as long as they do not attack the base root of the system—production and consumption. Therefore, the New Left activist who does not produce economic goods and who is consciously concerned with cutting down on his consumption of unnecessary goods is a direct threat to the system. He must be attacked. Freedom is undesirable in a capitalist system. The only freedoms that can be assumed within the system are those which either do not affect production and consumption or have a positive effect upon it. The Marxian analysis was similar to this New Left analysis. The only differences are fairly minor and are due to the existence of a relatively affluent society today.

In these ways the New Left critique of contemporary society is the Marxian analysis. The solution to contemporary problems is not drawn as directly from Marxism, but there are some important similarities. One of these similarities is found in the notion of revolution. Marx believed that revolution would probably be necessary to change capitalist society into a more humane society. The New Left also believes that revolution will probably be necessary. It will probably be necessary for the simple reason that the capitalists will be unwilling to change. They will be unwilling to give up what they have now for a society in which there is freedom, equality, and community.

Most of the New Left believes that capitalism must be replaced by a system based upon community which, in most cases leads them to the conclusion that some form of socialism is the best system. In discussing the economic system, I said that the work situation was to be controlled by the workers and the economic system in general was to be community-controlled. This is what the New Left means when it uses the word "socialism."

The communes today generally have community of goods; this seems to be broadly accepted on the New Left. Thus it seems reasonable to assume that the distribution system would be based on individual need through communally held property rather than on different monetary rewards for different services. Still, the New Left is not very clear on this point and the use of the term "socialism" is not specific enough to allow one to conclude much about the distributional aspects of the desired economy.

What makes it possible to draw some conclusions about the distribution system is the role of community and equality in New Left thought. Freedom does not mean freedom for differential reward in money. Freedom is based upon community and security, including economic security, within the community. Freedom, it is argued, cannot exist without community and equality. Therefore, it seems fair to conclude that the distribution of economic goods in the future society would be on the basis of need within a community context and hence would probably be fairly equal. Demonstrable differential need would be taken care of within the community. But it is likely that the focus would be on individual need rather than family or subgroup need so that differential treatment will be based on individual differences rather than differences in some subgroup of the community. Economic decisions of this sort will be made in exactly the same way as other decisions—agreement among all participating members of the community.

In summary then, the debts of the New Left to the tradition of Marxian Socialism may be seen as follows:

1. The concept of alienation.
2. Much of the content of the critique of contemporary society based upon the rejection of capitalism and competition.
3. The notion of revolution as necessary to change capitalism.
4. The symbol of socialism as a means of organizing the economy of the future society.

At the same time, certain parts of the Marxian analysis and most of the Communist practice have been rejected. Some of these rejections are:

1. The philosophical underpinning of Marx found in materialism and the dialectic.
2. Much of the class analysis found in Marx.
3. The notion of state socialism found in contemporary Communist practice.

Marx's vision of a future society in which equality, liberty, and community are established is important to the New Left, but the New Left vision follows more closely the anarchist model. The debts of the New Left to anarchism are both more obvious and less known than the debts to Marxian socialism. They are less known because anarchism is less known. They are quite clear when both anarchism and the New Left are compared. Anarchism may be characterized as follows:

1. Strongest emphasis on freedom—no government.
2. Concern with basic equality, usually provided through socialism.[3]
3. Decision-making by consensual agreement of the whole community, but:
   a. Individual assumed to be free to disregard the decision.
   b. Spontaneous cooperation assumed.
4. Workers' control.
5. Decentralization.
6. Need for revolution.

The differences between anarchism and the New Left are primarily ones of emphasis rather than kind.

The central focus of anarchism is on freedom and particularly the freedom that will come about as a result of the disappearance of government, that is, the disappearance of coercion. While this is a strong element in New Left thought, it is not necessarily the most important element, whereas in anarchism it is the most important. Therefore there is one basic difference between anarchism and the New Left, but I think that it should be understood that the difference is clearly one of emphasis rather than one of kind. Both agree that in most circumstances, government, coercive authority, must be done away with and replaced by a decision-making system based on participation. Therefore it can be seen that in this basic goal the similarities are very great.

---

[3] There are exceptions—the individualist anarchists and the capitalist anarchists being the major ones.

The notion of community is of importance to both the New Left and to anarchism, but it seems to be of more central importance to the New Left. I have shown that the establishment of close interpersonal relations in a community is one of the main goals of the New Left. While it is an important element in anarchism, the emphasis is on the individual rather than the community. The New Left of course sees the community as benefiting the individual, but the focus is on the relationship within communities rather than on the individual.

The distinction made here between the community and the individual is a bit sharper than either anarchism or the New Left would accept, but it is important to draw the line clearly between the two in this area. While they both see the individual in a social context and do not clearly separate the two, the focus is as I've stated it—anarchism leans slightly toward the individual and the New Left slightly toward the community.

Also, the process of community decision-making is of much greater concern to the New Left than it is to anarchism. The New Left, particularly in its concept of participatory democracy, is deeply concerned with the difficulties of reaching decisions within a community. Anarchism, although it recognizes the problems, is not as concerned with them. Anarchism focuses on the process of cooperation that can come out of a community situation and tends to slide over the difficulties. The New Left focuses directly on this process of decision-making.

These differences, although important, should not obscure the more significant similarities. I noted the emphasis on workers' control, decentralization, and revolution in anarchism. These points are exactly the same in the New Left.

The anarchist's greater emphasis on the individual is found in the New Left in its consideration of some aspects of society such as the educational system, changes in the family system and sexual relationships, and changes in the mass media.

The New Left is concerned with developing the greatest possible amount of freedom for individuals to practice various life styles and modes of behavior. This may take forms such as the differing sexual practices that shock so many today, or the milder revolts in clothes and hair length. The importance attached to these both by contemporary society and the New Left is instructive. The New Left views the clothes and hair styles as minor elements of revolt and identification and as symbolic of new life styles and new patterns of behavior. Contemporary society seems to perceive them solely as revolts against itself.

Such things as changed sexual relationships are direct attempts to overcome the alienation and the hypocrisy connected with contemporary sexual practices. Whether or not laying the blame on the specific concern with sex found in contemporary society is correct or not does not really matter. What is important is that these changed sexual relationships are seen by the New Left, or at least significant segments of it, as being important changes in life style *now* that reflect the lines of the future society. By moving away from individual sex partners to group sex or at least experimenting with different forms of sexual relationships such as group sex, either bisexual or heterosexual, or homosexual relations, the New Left, and many people who are picking up the ideas of the New Left in this area, are attempting to find some sort of community in very close interpersonal relations. They are also trying to find how they may overcome their own alienation and find greater fulfillment and greater self-identification.

These changes in sexual relations are also important for other reasons. First, they are a direct rejection of the hypocrisy regarding sex found in contemporary society. Second, they contain a recognition of sexual pleasure and pleasure in general. And, finally, they are a recognition that sexual pleasure and pleasure in general may be found in a variety of forms that are not approved of by contemporary society. The sexual example is the most important for the changes that are taking place today. Not all of the people participating in these changes could be identified with the New Left, but most of the younger people who are participating do make that identification to some extent. Even if they are not activists or dropouts, they seem to make that identification symbolically through clothes, hair length, and the argot they use. This identification may bring about a greater identification with the more specific political goals of the New Left in the future, since identification at one level can easily lead to identification at other levels.

The changes in sexual relationships are conceived by many to be part of the revolution and part of the future society. It is possible now to practice things that are not approved by contemporary society, and these things, it is felt, are what *should* be the ideal way of life. Pleasure is good; it should be found wherever possible.

It is possible to see some of the emphasis on pleasure as coming *from* the alienation rather than from the overcoming of alienation. The search for pleasure has traditionally been seen as a rather desperate search for something to overcome the horrors of everyday life. This may be true to some extent, but it seems to be less true today than in the past. Pleasure is seen as something good, something desirable, and something that should be sought in and of itself, not directly as an attempt to overcome something else. Thus the ethos of the New Left, and those who identify with them, is a pleasure ethos. It is one that is concerned with the here and now, with the full life now, and a full life is one that includes significant amounts of pleasure.

Contemporary society is seen as pleasure-denying. The society of the future is seen as pleasure-enhancing. Anarchism has traditionally held similar views. It has been in the forefront of sexual reform and has generally been pleasure-enhancing. The revolt against limitations of pleasure—and specifically limitations on sexual practices—is parallel to similar revolts of anarchists through the centuries.

Both anarchism and the New Left see as good that which is pleasurable and that which helps to fulfill the human being. Both see as good the expression of individual freedom in revolts against a pleasure-denying society and revolts against contemporary hypocrisy. Anarchists have been the traditional leaders in this type of revolt. The New Left has taken over this role.

Another area in which anarchism has been on the forefront of attempts to free institutions has been in the educational system. Most of the ideas of the New Left on education which I discussed were expressed earlier by anarchists or those who partially identified themselves with anarchism. Anarchists have always been concerned with the problem of education for freedom and have always been in the forefront of those criticizing contemporary educational institutions as limiting of freedom rather than freedom-enhancing. Again there is a clear parallel between anarchism and the New Left.

In another social institution, the family, anarchists have played a similar role. Anarchists have always argued that relationships should be made by choice of individuals rather than through meeting the sanction of either religion or state, and the New Left has moved to this position also.

Regarding religion specifically, anarchism is less diverse than the New Left and those connected with it. Anarchism seems to contain two very unequal divisions. On the one hand, there is the overwhelming majority who believe that anarchism and religion are incompatible or at least that anarchism and any organized religion are incompatible, that no individual should accept from any source a belief or doctrine that is not his own. This argument rejects the notion that religion can be defined by an organization and accepted by an individual. The development of religious belief must be personal, independent, and individual. On the other hand, there are numbers of Christian anarchists, and specifically Catholic anarchists, who dispute this view. The view held by such Christian anarchists is that religious belief can be defined by a church and accepted and believed by an individual. What they reject are attempts by a church to deal with questions of society and politics. The similarities among these anarchists seem greater than the differences because both reject governmental institutions and any religious institution that concerns itself with anything but narrowly defined religious questions.

As I noted, the New Left has connected to it, or at least parallel to it, a wide variety of religious groups that identify at least in part with some of the new counter-culture. While these are not co-extensive with the New Left, they are certainly intimately entwined with it—and it seems that this is likely to continue to be so in the future. I noted that this religious diversity seems to be directly connected with the search for the authentic self, which is a peculiar attribute of the New Left and not found as significantly or emphasized as much in any of the other political philosophies that are similar to the New Left.

The search for the authentic self may be particularly important to the New Left because of the large element of youth in it who traditionally go through a period of such search and are concerned with the problems of such a search in a society that limits the options so greatly. In this way, too, there is a parallel to anarchism. The anarchist argues that no individual can be wholly himself in a coercive society. The New Left makes the same point but uses different terms. No individual can find himself without the freedom to experiment with a variety of life styles and a variety of life situations.

Thus the goals of the New Left and the goals of anarchism are basically the same. Both anarchism and the New Left emphasize the concept of freedom. The differences are found in the greater emphasis on community for the New Left as opposed to the greater emphasis on freedom for anarchism. The New Left is, also, more concerned with decision-making within the community than is anarchism.

The greatest difference, though, may be in the New Left's concern with a period of transition. Anarchism rarely deals with what happens as society gradually changes. Even if a revolution is successful, it is not likely to bring about the complete transformation of society within a very brief period of time, but most anarchist pictures of revolution and the period immediately thereafter deal with a rapid transformation. The New Left does not seem to accept this notion.

The New Left sees participatory democracy as both a means of reform and a means of organizing society in the future. The

New Left argues that everyone should be able to participate as much as possible now in the decisions that affect their lives, even though under contemporary circumstances they cannot participate as much as they will be able to in the future. And if a revolution succeeds, the New Left recognizes that there would be a period of adjustment—one in which participatory democracy would be an important means of meeting the problems. The ability of each individual to participate in the decisions made during the period of transition after a revolution would ideally mean that all points of view would be protected.

But at the same time, the New Left does seem to believe, as does anarchism and as did Marx, that the revolution itself will transform men greatly, that men will become much more cooperative beings simply by being part of a revolution. The destruction of competitive society is seen as a process of enlightenment, a process of individual transformation, and as a major means of overcoming alienation and finding the true self. This approach to revolution is important for understanding the belief that anarchists hold that a non-coercive society can be established immediately after the revolution, and it is also important for understanding the New Left's belief that the transformation after the revolution will not be particularly difficult.

But the New Left recognizes that the transformation will not be instantaneous, and that it will not be easy. The New Left believes that the decision-making procedures found in participatory democracy will make the transformation possible. It may be necessary during a period of transition to do away gradually with levels of government (until neighborhoods are established or new communities are founded), and thus it may be necessary to have some government—but under the much more direct control of the people than exists now. The New Left has not dealt with these problems specifically, and it would be inaccurate to say more than that it seems to have recognized problems which its anarchist forebears did not.

It is difficult to state the importance of the New Left with any certainty. Its members have a commitment to the values of Western civilization—values that they say have been lost today. They criticize contemporary society for its hypocrisy in ostensibly opposing racism and sexism but in actuality practicing them. They argue that the capitalist competitive system cannot overcome alienation, racism, sexism, and cannot produce a good, humane life for the majority of the people.

The New Left has pointed to a vision of the future society that has overcome alienation, racism, and sexism. In this book we have looked at this vision of the future society and seen some of the suggested lines that the New Left would like it to take.

We cannot ignore either the vision of the future society or the criticism that the New Left makes of contemporary society—not because society will collapse if we do, but because they express the values that we have always believed in and have always believed that we were putting into practice.

The New Left suggests that we review our priorities and attempt to change. We could, for example, note the value of participation in the political realm and attempt to open up our institutions today to include more participation by more people. We say we value participation, but we do not have it, and we do not seem to be particularly concerned with getting it. The New Left points to this and says that we are hypocrites.

We could make serious attempts to overcome racism, sexism, and inequality in general. We seem to be unwilling to do so. We pay lip service to equality and say that we are proceeding toward it. But we are in fact doing very little.

We could encourage diversity, we could encourage new ideas and new ways of life rather than trying to maintain a narrow rigidity of the past. It is certainly not demonstrable that a variety of life styles is bad. We do not know. We are supposedly dedicated to freedom, the right to express oneself, and the right of each individual to fulfill himself, but we are unwilling to guarantee these rights if doing so permits deviance from our customs and conventions. Again, we are being narrow and hypocritical.

The foregoing was written from the point of view of one who believes that reform is both necessary and possible. Looked at from a slightly different perspective, however, the New Left can be seen as becoming more and more dedicated to the proposition that society as it exists today must be destroyed if it will not change. The New Left is dedicated to revolutionizing contemporary society. Whether it does it within the terms of the political and social structure as it is now, or within a different structure, it is concerned with ending the capitalist system as soon as possible. It says that capitalism is incapable of producing a humane society. Capitalism has certainly not yet demonstrated that it can. It is a simple fact that more and more young people today are dedicating themselves to radically transforming society, and for this reason, if for no other, we *must* look at ourselves and our society. We cannot simply respond that we are right and they are wrong; we must *look* at what we are and what we do and then decide whether or not those on the New Left are correct in their charges. A society that produces professional revolutionaries, activists dedicated to a long-term revolution to overthrow the country, reformers who believe that revolution is ultimately necessary, and thousands of youth who simply drop out would seem to stand in need of self-scrutiny.

BIBLIOGRAPHY

The following bibliography attempts to indicate the variety of places in which the literature of the New Left is found. It is somewhat long because of the lack of a good bibliography on the New Left. Almost all of the books listed are available in paperback. Although articles from Movement journals are not listed, titles of some of the journals are included at the end.

The old left

Out of the vast literature the following are particularly useful for providing a general overview.

Beer, Max. *The General History of Socialism and Social Struggles.* 5 Vols. in 2. New York: Russell & Russell, 1957.

Cole, G. D. H. *A History of Socialist Thought.* 5 Vols. in 7. London: Macmillan, 1953–60.

Egbert, Donald Drew, and Stow Persons (eds.). *Socialism and American Life.* 2 Vols. Princeton, N.J.: Princeton University Press, 1952.

Fried, Albert. *Socialism in America from the Shakers to the Third International: A Documentary History.* Garden City, N.Y.: Anchor Books, 1970.

————, and Ronald Sanders (eds.). *Socialist Thought: A Documentary History.* Garden City, N.Y.: Anchor Books, 1964.

Gray, Alexander. *The Socialist Tradition.* London: Longmans, Green & Co., 1946.

Howe, Irving (ed.). *Essential Works of Socialism.* New York: Bantam Books, 1970.

Huberman, Leo, and Paul M. Sweezy. *Introduction to Socialism.* New York: Modern Reader Paperbacks, 1968.

Laidler, Harry W. *History of Socialism.* London: Routledge & Kegan Paul, 1969.

MacKenzie, Norman. *Socialism: A Short History*. Rev. ed. London: Hutchinson University Library, 1966.

Meyer, Alfred G. *Communism*. 3d ed. New York: Random House, 1967.

Quint, Howard H. *The Forging of American Socialism*. Indianapolis, Ind.: The Bobbs-Merrill Co., 1953.

Existentialism

Aron, Raymond. *Marxism and the Existentialists*. New York: Simon & Schuster, 1969.

Barrett, William. *Irrational Man: A Study in Existential Philosophy*. Garden City, N.Y.: Doubleday & Co., 1958.

Burnier, Michel Antoine. *Choice of Action: The French Existentialists on the Political Front Line*. trans. Bernard Murchland. New York: Random House, 1968.

Camus, Albert. *The Rebel: An Essay on Man in Revolt*. trans. Anthony Bower. New York: Vintage Books, 1956.

―――. *Resistance, Rebellion, and Death*. trans. Justin O'Brien. New York: Alfred A. Knopf, 1960.

Desan, Wilfrid. *The Marxism of Jean-Paul Sartre*. Garden City, N.Y.: Doubleday, 1965.

Odajynk, Walter. *Marxism and Existentialism*. Garden City, N.Y.: Doubleday, 1965.

Parker, Emmett. *Albert Camus: The Artist in the Arena*. Madison: University of Wisconsin Press, 1965.

Sartre, Jean-Paul. *Existentialism*. trans. Bernard Frechtman. New York: Philosophical Library, 1947.

Willhoite, Fred H., Jr. *Beyond Nihilism: Albert Camus's Contribution to Political Thought*. Baton Rouge: Louisiana State University Press, 1968.

The background of the movement

Aptheker, Herbert. *Documentary History of the Negro People in the United States*. 2 Vols. New York: Citadel Press, 1951.

Aron, Raymond. *The Elusive Revolution: Anatomy of a Student Revolt*. London: Pall Mall Press, 1969.

Bellasci, Pietro. *Rivolta Studentesca e Campus Universitari*. Milano Angeli Editore, 1968.

Brisbane, Robert H. *The Black Vanguard: Origins of the Negro Social Revolution, 1900–1960*. Valley Forge, Pa.: Judson, 1970.

Broderick, Francis L., and August Meier (eds.).   *Negro Protest*

Thought in the Twentieth Century. Indianapolis, Ind.: The Bobbs-Merrill Co., 1965.

Brotz, Howard (ed.). *Negro Social and Political Thought 1850–1920: Representative Texts.* New York: Basic Books, 1966.

Burns, W. Haywood. *The Voices of Negro Protest in America.* New York: Oxford University Press, 1963.

Califano, Joseph A., Jr. *The Student Revolution: A Global Confrontation.* New York: W. W. Norton, 1970.

Catalano, Franco. *I Movimenti Studenteschi e la Scuola in Italia (1938–1968).* Milano: il Saggiatore di Alberto Mondadori Editore, 1969.

Cohn-Bendit, Daniel, et al. *The French Student Revolt: The Leaders Speak.* New York: Hill & Wang, 1968.

Colombo, Arrigo. *Università e rivoluzione.* Manduria: Lacaita editore, 1970.

Combats étudiants dans le monde. Paris: Editions du Seuil, 1968.

Draper, Hal. *Berkeley: The New Student Revolt.* New York: Grove Press, 1965.

Ehrenreich, Barbara, and John Ehrenreich. *Long March, Short Spring: The Student Uprising at Home and Abroad.* New York: Monthly Review Press, 1969.

Feuer, Lewis S. *The Conflict of Generations: The Character and Significance of Student Movements.* New York: Basic Books, 1969.

Glazer, Nathan. *Remembering the Answers: Essays on the American Student Revolt.* New York: Basic Books, 1970.

Gomez, Raffaele. *Università; Il Nocciolo della Crisi.* L'Aquila: Japadre Editore, 1969.

Hansberry, Lorraine. *The Movement: Documentary of a Struggle for Equality.* New York: Simon & Schuster, 1964.

Horowitz, David. *Student.* New York: Ballantine Books, 1962.

Hughes, Langston. *The Story of the NAACP.* New York: W. W. Norton. 1962.

Jack, Robert L. *History of the National Association for the Advancement of Colored People.* Boston: Meador Publishing Co., 1943.

Kerouac, Jack. *The Dharma Bums.* New York: New American Library, 1958.

———. *On the Road.* New York: New American Library, 1957.

King, Martin Luther, Jr. *Strength to Love.* New York: Harper & Row, 1958.

———. *Stride Toward Freedom.* New York: Harper & Row, 1953.

————. *Where Do We Go From Here? Chaos or Community*. Boston: Beacon Press, 1967.

————. *Why We Can't Wait*. New York: Harper & Row, 1963.

Lefebvre, Henri. *The Explosion: Marxism and the French Revolution*. trans. Alfred Ehrenfeld. New York: Monthly Review Press, 1969. Original title: *L'Irruption de Nanterre au sommet*.

Lewis, Anthony, and *The New York Times*. *Portrait of a Decade: The Second American Revolution*. New York: Random House, 1964.

Lipset, Seymour Martin, and Sheldon S. Wolin (eds.). *The Berkeley Student Revolt: Facts and Interpretations*. Garden City, N.Y.: Doubleday, 1965.

————, and Philip G. Altbach (eds.). *Students in Revolt*. Boston: Houghton Mifflin, 1969. Originally published as the Winter 1968 issue of *Daedalus*.

Lipton, Lawrence. *The Holy Barbarians*. New York: Julian Messner, 1959.

Lomax, Louis E. *The Negro Revolt*. New York: Harper & Row, 1962.

Louis, Debbie. *And We Are Not Saved: A History of the Movement as People*. Garden City, N.Y.: Doubleday, 1970.

Lynd, Staughton (ed.). *Nonviolence in America: A Documentary History*. Indianapolis, Ind.: Bobbs-Merrill, 1966.

Masotti, Louis H., et al. *A Time to Burn? An Evaluation of the Present Crisis in Race Relations*. Chicago: Rand McNally, 1969.

Miller, Michael V., and Susan Gilmore (eds.). *Revolution in Berkeley*. New York: Dell, 1965.

Muse, Benjamin. *The American Negro Revolution: From Nonviolence to Black Power, 1963–1967*. Bloomington: Indiana University Press, 1968.

————. *Ten Years of Prelude: The Story of Integration Since the Supreme Court's 1954 Decision*. New York: Viking Press, 1964.

Nagel, Julian (ed.). *Student Power*. London: Merlin Press, 1969.

Niel, Mathilde. *Le Mouvement étudiant ou la révolution en marche; Signification du mouvement étudiant contemporaine*. Paris: Le Courrier du livre, 1968.

Oliva, Carlo, and Aloisio Rendi. *Il movimento studentesco el le sue lotte*. Milano: Feltrinelli Editore, 1969.

Parkinson, Thomas F. *A Casebook on the Beats*. New York: Crowell, 1961.

Rooke, Margaret Anne. *Anarchy and Apathy: Student Unrest 1968–1970*. London: Hamish Hamilton, 1971.

Seale, Patrick, and Maureen McConville. *French Revolution 1968*. London and Harmondsworth: William Heinemann and Penguin, 1968.

Silberman, Charles. *Crisis in Black and White*. New York: Random House, 1964.

Spender, Stephen. *The Year of the Young Rebels*. New York: Random House, 1969.

Storing, Herbert J. (ed.). *What Country Have I? Political Writings by Black Americans*. New York: St. Martin's Press, 1970.

Warshaw, Steven. *The Trouble in Berkeley*. Berkeley, Calif.: Diablo Press, 1965.

Young, Richard P. (ed.). *Roots of Rebellion: The Evolution of Black Politics and Protest Since World War II*. New York: Harper & Row, 1970.

Young, Whitney. *To Be Equal*. New York: McGraw-Hill, 1964.

Zinn, Howard. *SNCC: The New Abolitionists*. Boston: Beacon Press, 1965.

The movement—general works and collections

Abcarian, Gilbert (ed.). *American Political Radicalism: Contemporary Issues and Orientations*. Waltham, Mass.: Xerox College Publishing, 1971.

Anderson, Albert, and Bernice Prince Biggs (eds.). *A Focus on Rebellion*. San Francisco: Chandler Publishing Co., 1962.

Anderson, Walt (ed.). *The Age of Protest*. Pacific Palisades, Calif.: Goodyear Publishing Co., 1969.

Aronson, Ronald, and John C. Cowley. "The New Left in the United States," *The Socialist Register 1967*, Ralph Miliband and Saville (eds.). New York: Monthly Review Press, 1967, pp. 73–90.

Aya, Roderick, and Norman Miller (eds.). *The New American Revolution*. New York: The Free Press, 1971.

Baran, Paul A., and Paul M. Sweezy. *Monopoly Capital: An Essay on the American Economic and Social Order*. New York: Monthly Review Press, 1966.

Benello, C. G., and D. Roussopoulos (eds.). *The Case for Participatory Democracy: Some Prospects for the Radical Society*. New York: Grossman, 1971.

Berger, Peter L., and Richard John Neuhaus. *Movement and Revolution*. Garden City, N.Y.: Anchor Books, 1970.

Berube, Maurice R., and Marilyn Gettell (eds.). *Confrontation at Ocean Hill-Brownsville*. New York: Praeger, 1969.

Buckman, Peter. *The Limits of Protest*. Indianapolis, Ind.: Bobbs-Merrill, 1970.

Casale, Ottavio, and Louis Paskoff (eds.). *The Kent Affair: Documents and Interpretations*. Boston: Houghton Mifflin, 1971.

Chicago Eight. *Conspiracy*. New York: Dell Publishing Co., 1969.

Chomsky, Noam. *American Power and The New Mandarins*. New York: Pantheon Books, 1969.

Cohen, Mitchell, and Dennis Hale (eds.). *The New Student Left: An Anthology*. Rev. and enl. ed. Boston: Beacon Press, 1967.

Cohn-Bendit, Daniel, and Gabriel Cohn-Bendit. *Obsolete Communism: The Left-Wing Alternative*. trans. Arnold Pomerans. London: André-Deutsch, 1968.

Cook, Terrence E., and Patrick M. Morgan (eds.). *Participatory Democracy*. San Francisco: Canfield Press, 1971. Has a good bibliography.

Cooper, David (ed.). *To Free a Generation: The Dialectics of Liberation*. New York: Collier Books, 1968.

Cranston, Maurice (ed.). *The New Left: Six Critical Essays*. London: The Bodley Head, 1970.

Crick, Bernard, and William A. Robson (eds.). *Protest and Discontent*. Baltimore: Penguin Books, Ltd., 1970.

Dahl, Robert A. *After the Revolution? Authority in A Good Society*. New Haven, Conn.: Yale University Press, 1970.

Editors of *Ramparts*. *Conversations With the New Reality: Readings in the Cultural Revolution*. San Francisco: Canfield Press, 1971.

———. *Divided We Stand*. San Francisco: Canfield Press, 1970.

Erlich, John, and Susan Erlich (eds.). *Student Power, Participation and Revolution*. New York: Association Press, 1970.

Esfandiary, F. M. *Optimism One: The Emerging Radicalism*. New York: W. W. Norton, 1970.

Feigelson, Naomi. *The Underground Revolution: Hippies, Yippies and Others*. New York: Funk & Wagnalls, 1970.

Fischer, George (ed.). *The Revival of American Socialism: Selected Papers of the Socialist Scholars Conference*. New York: Oxford University Press, 1971.

Gerberding, William P., and Duane E. Smith (eds.). *The Radical Left: The Abuse of Discontent*. Boston: Houghton Mifflin, 1970.

Golembiewski, Robert T., Charles S. Bullock III, and Harrell R. Rodgers, Jr. *The New Politics: Polarization or Utopia?* New York: McGraw-Hill, 1970.

Goodman, Mitchell (comp.). *The Movement Toward a New America: The Beginnings of a Long Revolution (A Collage) A What? 1. A Comprehension 2. A Compendium 3. A Handbook 4. A Guide 5. A History 6. A Revolution Kit 7. A Work-In-Progress.* Philadelphia and New York: Pilgrim Press and Alfred A. Knopf, 1970.

Goodman, Paul, and Percival Goodman. *Communitas: Means of Livlihood and Ways of Life.* New York: Vintage Books, 1960.

————. *Growing Up Absurd: Problems of Youth in the Organized System.* New York: Random House, 1960.

Gray, Francine du Plessix. *Divine Disobedience: Profiles in Catholic Radicalism.* New York: Vintage Books, 1970.

Guevara, Ernesto Che. *Che Guevara on Guerilla Warfare.* New York: Praeger, 1961.

Hamalian, Leo, and Frederick R. Karl (eds.). *The Radical Vision: Essays for the Seventies.* New York: Thomas Y. Crowell, 1970.

Harrington, Michael. *Toward a Democratic Left: A Radical Program for a New Majority.* New York: Macmillan, 1968.

Hayden, Tom. *Rebellion and Repression.* New York: Meridian Books, 1969.

————. *Trial.* New York: Holt, Rinehart & Winston, 1970.

Hendel, Samuel (ed.). *The Politics of Confrontation.* New York: Appleton-Century-Crofts, 1971.

Hoffman, Abbie. *Revolution for the Hell of It,* by Free (pseud.). New York: Dial, 1968.

————. *Woodstock Nation: A Talk-Rock Album.* New York: Vintage Books, 1969.

Horowitz, Irving Louis. *Struggle Is the Message: The Anti-War Movement.* Berkeley, Calif.: Glendessary Press, Inc., 1970.

Howe, Irving. *Steady Work: Essays in the Politics of Democratic Radicalism 1953–1966.* New York: Harcourt, Brace and World, 1966.

Jacobs, Harold (ed.). *Weatherman.* Np.: Ramparts Press, 1970.

Jacobs, Paul, and Saul Landau. *The New Radicals: A Report with Documents.* New York: Vintage Books, 1966.

Jaffe, Harold, and John Tytell (eds.). *The American Experience: A Radical Reader.* New York: Harper and Row, 1970.

Keniston, Kenneth. *Young Radicals: Notes on Committed Youth.* New York: Harcourt, Brace and Jovanovich, 1968.

Kolko, Gabriel. *The Decline of American Radicalism in the Twentieth Century.* Boston: New England Free Press, nd. Pamphlet.

Kornbluth, Jesse (ed.). *Notes from the New Underground: An Anthology.* New York: The Viking Press, 1968.

Kostelanetz, Richard (ed.). *Beyond Right and Left: Radical Thought for Our Times.* New York: William Morrow, 1968.

Kunen, James Simon. *The Strawberry Statement: Notes of a College Revolutionary.* New York: Random House, 1968.

Laing, R. D. *The Politics of Experience.* New York: Ballantine Books, 1967.

Lasch, Christopher. *The Agony of the American Left.* New York: Random House, 1966.

Lauter, Paul, and Florence Howe. *The Conspiracy of the Young.* New York: World Publishing Co., 1970.

Long, Priscilla (ed.). *The New Left: A Collection of Essays.* Boston: Porter Sargent Publisher, 1969.

Lothstein, Arthur (ed.). *"All We are Saying . . .": The Philosophy of the New Left.* New York: Capricorn Books, 1970.

Lutz, William, and Harry Brent (eds.). *On Revolution.* Cambridge, Mass.: Winthrop Publishers, Inc., 1971.

Lynd, Alice (ed.). *We Won't Go.* Boston: Beacon Press, 1968.

Marcuse, Herbert. *Eros and Civilization: A Philosophical Inquiry into Freud.* Boston: Beacon Press, 1955.

―――. *An Essay on Liberation.* Boston: Beacon Press, 1969.

―――. *Five Lectures: Psychoanalysis, Politics, and Utopia.* trans. Jeremy J. Shapiro and Shierry M. Weber. Boston: Beacon Press, 1970.

―――. *Negations: Essays in Critical Theory.* trans. Jeremy J. Shapiro. Boston: Beacon Press, 1968.

―――. *One-Dimensional Man: Studies in the Ideology of Advanced Industrial Society.* Boston: Beacon Press, 1964.

Muller, Robert H., et al. (eds.). *From Radical Left to Extreme Right.* 2d ed. Ann Arbor: Campus Publishers, 1970.

Myerson, Michael. *These Are the Good Old Days: Coming of Age As a Radical in America's Late, Late Years.* New York: Grossmann Publishers, 1970.

Neill, A. S. *Summerhill: A Radical Approach to Child Rearing.* New York: Hart, 1960.

Newfield, Jack. *A Prophetic Minority.* New York: New American Library, 1966.

Oglesby, Carl, and Richard Shaull. *Containment and Change.* New York: Macmillan, 1967.

—— (ed.). *The New Left Reader.* New York: Grove Press, Inc., 1969.

Otto, Herbert A. (ed.). *The Family in Search of a Future: Alternate Models for Moderns.* New York: Appleton-Century-Crofts, 1970.

Powell, William. *The Anarchist Cookbook.* New York: Lyle Stuart, 1971.

Reich, Charles A. *The Greening of America.* New York: Random House, 1970.

Rimmer, Robert H. *The Harrad Experiment.* New York: Bantam Books, 1966.

——. *Proposition 31.* New York: New American Library, 1968.

Romm, Ethel Grodzins. *The Open Conspiracy: What America's Angry Generation is Saying.* New York: K. S. Gininger & Co., 1970.

Roszak, Theodore. *The Making of a Counter Culture: Reflections on the Technocratic Society and Its Youthful Opposition.* Garden City: Doubleday & Co., Inc., 1969. Has a useful bibliography.

Rubin, Jerry. *Do It! Scenarios of the Revolution.* New York: Simon & Schuster, 1970.

——. *We Are Everywhere.* New York: Harper and Row, 1971.

Silverman, Henry J. (ed.). *American Radical Thought: The Libertarian Tradition.* Lexington, Mass.: D.C. Heath & Co., 1970. Has an excellent bibliography.

Slater, Philip E. *The Pursuit of Loneliness: American Culture at the Breaking Point.* Boston: Beacon Press, 1970.

Teodori, Massimo (ed.). *The New Left: A Documentary History.* Indianapolis, Ind.: The Bobbs-Merrill Co., Inc., 1969.

von Hoffman, Nicholas. *We Are the People Our Parents Warned Us Against.* Greenwich, Conn.: Fawcett Publications, Inc., 1968.

Wolfe, Tom. *The Electric Kool-Aid Acid Test.* New York: Bantam Books, 1968.

Young, Alfred F. (ed.). *Dissent: Explorations in the History of American Radicalism.* DeKalb, Ill.: Northern Illinois University Press, 1968.

Zorza, Richard. *The Right to Say We: The Adventures of a Young Englishman at Harvard and in the Youth Movement.* New York: Praeger, 1970.

The communal movement

A. The tradition

Albertson, Ralph. "A Survey of Mutualistic Communities in America," *Iowa Journal of History and Politics,* Vol. 34 (July 1936), pp. 375–444.

Armytage, W. H. G. *Heavens Below: Utopian Experiments in England 1560–1960.* London: Routledge & Kegan Paul, 1961.

Bach, Marcus. *Strange Sects and Curious Cults.* New York: Dodd, Mead, 1961.

Bestor, Arthur Eugene, Jr. *Backwoods Utopias: The Sectarian and Owenite Phases of Communitarian Socialism in America 1663–1829.* 2d enl. ed. Philadelphia: University of Pennsylvania Press, 1970.

Bishop, Claire Huchet. *All Things Common.* New York: Harper, 1950.

Bushee, Frederick A. "Communistic Societies in the United States," *Political Science Quarterly,* Vol. 20 (December 1905), pp. 625–64.

Calverton, Victor Francis. *Where Angels Dared to Tread: Socialist and Communistic Utopian Colonies in the United States.* Freeport, N.Y.: Books for Libraries Press, 1969. Originally published in 1941.

Clark, Elmer T. *The Small Sects in America.* Nashville, Tenn.: Cokesbury Press, 1937.

Gide, Charles. *Communistic and Co-operative Colonies.* trans. Ernest F. Row. New York: Thomas Y. Crowell, 1930.

Hinds, William Alfred. *American Communities.* New York: Corinth, 1961. Reprint of the 1878 edition. The editions of 1902 and 1908 were more extensive.

Hine, Robert V. *California's Utopian Colonies.* San Marino, Calif.: Huntington Library, 1953.

Holloway, Mark. *Heavens on Earth: Utopian Communities in America 1680–1880.* New York: Library Publishers, 1951.

Kent, Rev. Alexander. "Cooperative Communities in the United States," *Bulletin of the Department of Labor,* Vol. 6 (July 1901), pp. 563–646.

Nordhoff, Charles. *The Communistic Societies of the United States.* New York: Hillary House, 1961. Originally published in 1874.

Noyes, John Humphrey. *History of American Socialisms.* New York: Hillary House, 1961. Originally published in 1870.

Wooster, Ernest S. *Communities of the Past and Present.* Newllano, La.: Llano *Colonist,* 1924.

Zablocki, Benjamin. *The Joyful Community.* Baltimore: Penguin, 1971.

B. The Kibbutzim

Ben-Yosef, Avraham C. *The Purest Democracy in the World.* London: Herzl Press and Thomas Yoseloff, 1963.

Bettelheim, Bruno. *The Children of the Dream: Communal Child-Rearing and American Education.* New York: Macmillan, 1969.

Darin-Drabkin, Haim. *The Other Society.* New York: Harcourt, Brace, & Co., 1963.

Kanovsky, Eliyahu. *The Economy of the Israeli Kibbutz.* Harvard Middle Eastern Monographs #XIII. Cambridge, Mass.: Harvard University Press, 1966.

Leon, Dan. *The Kibbutz: A New Way of Life.* Oxford: Pergamon Press, 1969.

Neubauer, Peter B. (ed.). *Children in Collectives: Child-rearing Aims and Practices in the Kibbutz.* Springfield, Ill.: Charles C. Thomas Publisher, 1965.

Rabin, Albert I. *Growing Up in the Kibbutz.* New York: Springer Publishing Co., 1965.

Spiro, Melford E. *Children of the Kibbutz.* Cambridge: Harvard University Press, 1958.

――――. *Kibbutz: Venture in Utopia.* 2d ed. New York: Schocken Books, 1963.

Stern, Boris. *The Kibbutz That Was.* Washington, D.C.: Public Affairs Press, 1965.

Weingarten, Murray. *Life in a Kibbutz.* Jerusalem: Zionest Organization, Youth and Hechalutz Department, 1959.

C. The new communalism

Outside and even inside the Movement press, the communal movement has been over-sensationalized, ignored, or romanticized. The best general approach to the new communes is through the pages of *The Modern Utopian, The Alternatives Newsletter, Alternate Society,* and *Communes.* In addition, many movement journals carry information on specific communes, and the best approach to this material is through the *Alternative Press Index. The Last Whole Earth Catalog* is also useful.

To keep my list as short as possible, and also because movement journals are only rarely available, the following includes only material outside the movement journals.

Lists of communities may be found in the following:

The Peacemaker, February 28, 1970, March 21, 1970, April 11, 1970.

The Modern Utopian, November, 1969, and most issues.

Ald, Roy. *The Youth Communes.* New York: Tower Publications, 1970. Poor.

Andrews, Lewis M. "Communes and the Work Crisis," *The Nation,* Vol. 211 (November 9, 1970), pp. 460–63.

Blumenthal, Ralph. "A Berlin Commune Is A Big Happy Family (Sometimes)," *New York Times Magazine,* December 1, 1968, pp. 52–3+.

"The Commune Comes to America," *Life,* Vol. 67 (July 18, 1969), pp. 16B–23.

Davidson, Sara. "Open Land: Getting Back to the Communal Garden," *Harper's Magazine,* Vol. 240 (June 1970), pp. 91–102. Comment: Vol. 241 (August 1970), pp. 6–8.

Fairfield, Dick. "Communes, USA," *The Modern Utopian,* Vol. 5, #'s 1–3 (1971). Will be published as a paperback by Penguin. The best survey so far.

Hedgepeth, William, and Dennis Stock. *The Alternative: Communal Life in New America.* New York: Macmillan, 1967.

Houriet, Robert. "Communing in Meadville," *Ramparts,* Vol. 7 (November 30, 1968), pp. 10–12.

———. "Life and Death of a Commune Called Oz," *New York Times Magazine,* February 16, 1969, pp. 30–31+. Comment: March 9, 1969, p. 12+.

Mead, Margaret. "Communes: A Challenge to Us All," *Redbook,* Vol. 135 (August 1970), pp. 51–52.

———. "New Designs for Family Living," *Redbook,* Vol. 135 (October 1970), pp. 22–25.

Otto, Herbert A. "Communes: The Alternative Life-Style," *Saturday Review,* Vol. 54 (April 24, 1971), pp. 16–21.

———. "Has Monogamy Failed?" *Saturday Review,* Vol. 53 (April 25, 1970), pp. 23–25+.

Rabbit, Peter. *Drop City.* New York: Olympia Press, 1971.

Robinson, Louie. "Life Inside a Hippie Commune," *Ebony*, Vol. 26 (November 1970), pp. 88–91+.

Rodale, Jerome Irving. "New Back to the Land Movement," *Organic Gardening and Farming*, Vol. 18 (May 1971). pp. 30–33.

———. "Young People, Are They America's New Peasantry?" *Organic Gardening and Farming*, Vol. 16 (September 1969), pp. 21–24.

Solnit, Albert. "Wear and Tear in the Communes," *The Nation*, Vol. 212 (April 26, 1971), pp. 524–27.

Spock, Benjamin. "Communes and Nurseries: Are They as Good for Children as They Are Helpful to Mothers?" *Redbook*, Vol. 135 (October 1970), pp. 28–33.

Stern, Sol. "Trouble in Paradise," *Ramparts*, Vol. 8 (November 1969), pp. 23–28.

Todd, Ralph. "'Walden Two' Three? Many More?" *New York Times Magazine*, March 15, 1970, pp. 24–25+.

White, Neal and Peter Schjeldahl. "Living High on the Hog Farm," *Avant Garde*, #5 (November 1968), pp. 44–51.

Zane, Maitland. "Living Together in California," *The Nation*, Vol. 211 (October 19, 1970), pp. 360–62.

Black radicalism

Barbour. Floyd B. (ed.). *The Black Power Revolt: A Collection of Essays*. Boston: Extending Horizons Books, 1968. Good bibliography.

Breitman, George (ed.). *Malcolm X Speaks: Selected Speeches and Statements*. New York: Grove Press, 1966.

Brown, H. Rap. *Die Nigger Die*. New York: Dial, 1969.

Carmichael, Stokely, and Charles V. Hamilton. *Black Power: The Politics of Liberation in America*. New York: Vintage Books, 1967.

Cleaver, Eldridge. *Post-Prison Writings and Speeches*, Robert Scheer (ed.). New York: Random House, 1969.

———. *Soul on Ice*. New York: Dell, 1968.

Epps, Archie (ed.). *The Speeches of Malcolm X at Harvard*. New York: William Morrow, 1968.

Essien-Udom, E. U. *Black Nationalism: A Search for an Identiy in America*. Chicago: University of Chicago Press, 1962.

Fanon, Frantz. *Black Skins, White Masks*. trans. Charles Lam Mackman. New York: Grove Press, 1967.

————. *A Dying Colonialism.* trans. Haakon Chevalier. New York: Grove Press, 1967.

————. *Toward the African Revolution (Political Essays).* trans. Haakon Chevalier. New York: Grove Press, 1967.

————. *The Wretched of the Earth.* trans. Constance Farrington. New York: Grove Press, 1968.

Foner, Philip S. (ed.). *The Black Panthers Speak.* Philadelphia: J. B. Lippincott, 1970.

Greenlee, Sam. *The Spook Who Sat By the Door.* New York: Bantam Books, 1969.

Greer, Edward. *Black Liberation Politics: A Reader.* Boston: Allyn and Bacon, Inc., 1971.

Grier, William H., and Price M. Cobbs. *Black Rage.* New York: Basic Books, 1968.

Killian, Lewis M. *The Impossible Revolution?: Black Power and the American Dream.* New York: Random House, 1968.

Lecky, Robert S., and H. Elliott Wright (eds.). *Black Manifesto: Religion, Racism, and Reparations.* New York: Sheed and Ward, 1969.

Lester, Julius. *Look Out, Whitey! Black Power's Gon' Get Your Mama!* New York: Dial Press, 1968.

————. *Revolutionary Notes.* New York: Richard W. Baron, 1969.

Lincoln, C. Eric. *Black Muslims in America.* Boston: Beacon Press, 1961.

McEvoy, James, and Abraham Miller (eds.). *Black Power and Student Rebellion.* Belmont, Calif.: Wadsworth, 1969.

Malcolm X. *The Autobiography of Malcolm X.* New York: Grove Press, 1964.

————. *By Any Means Necessary: Speeches, Interviews and a Letter,* George Breitman (ed.). New York: Pathfinder Press, 1970.

Marine, Gene. *The Black Panthers.* New York: New American Library, 1969.

Scott, Robert L., and Wayne Brockriede (eds.). *The Rhetoric of Black Power.* New York: Harper and Row, 1969.

Silverman, Sondra (ed.). *The Black Power Revolt and Democratic Politics.* Lexington, Mass.: D.C. Heath & Co., 1970.

Staff of Black Star Publishing (eds.). *The Political Thought of James Forman.* Detroit, Mich.: Black Star Publishing, 1970.

Truman, Nelson. *The Right of Revolution.* Boston: Beacon Press, 1968.

Williams, Robert. *Negroes With Guns*. New York: Marzani and Munsell, 1962.

The women's liberation movement

Since there is an excellent bibliography in Robin Morgan (ed.) *Sisterhood Is Powerful*, I have simply listed a few particularly important or interesting items and some other collections.

Bird, Caroline. *Born Female*. New York: McKay, 1968.
Cooke, Joanne, Charlotte Bunch-Weeks, and Robin Morgan (eds.). *The New Women: A MOTIVE Anthology on Women's Liberation*. Greenwich, Conn.: Fawcett Publications, Inc., 1970.
Firestone, Shulamith. *The Dialectic of Sex: The Case for Feminist Revolution*. New York: Bantam Books, 1970.
Hennessey, Caroline. *I, B.I.T.C.H.* New York: Lancer Books, 1970.
————. *The Strategy of Sexual Struggle*. New York: Lancer Books, 1971.
Jones, Beverly, and Judith Brown. *Toward a Female Liberation Movement*. Boston: New England Free Press, nd. Pamphlet.
McAfee, Kathy, and Myrna Wood. *What is the Revolutionary Potential of Women's Liberation?* Boston: New England Free Press, nd. Also entitled *Bread and Roses*. Pamphlet.
Mainardi, Pat. *The Politics of Housework*. Cambridge, Mass.: Betsy Warrior, nd. Pamphlet.
Millett, Kate. *Sexual Politics*. Garden City, N.Y.: Doubleday & Co., Inc., 1970.
Mitchell, Juliet. *Women's Estate*. Harmondsworth: Penguin, 1971.
Morgan, Robin (ed.). *Sisterhood Is Powerful: An Anthology of Writings from the Women's Liberation Movement*. New York: Random House, 1970.
Ware, Caroline. *Woman Power: The Movement for Women's Liberation*. New York: Tower Publications Inc., 1970.

Movement journals

The following is a fairly representative list of journals. They are now somewhat difficult to obtain, but they are being reprinted on microfilm and will undoubtedly be easier to find in the future. Additional lists of journals may be found in John R. Douglas, "Tribal Literature: Publications of the Counter Culture," *Wilson Library Bulletin*, Vol. 45 (December 1970), pp. 364–71, and in Len Fulton (ed.) *Little Magazines and Small Presses*, 6th ed. (Paradise, Calif.: Dustbooks, 1970). The latter lists underground newspapers, black publications, and G.I. anti-war papers in addition to little magazines and small presses.

Alternate Society
Alternatives Newsletter
Anarchos
Aphra
The Black Panther
Berkeley Tribe
CAW!
Communes, Journal of the Communal Movement
Despite Everything
Dissent
Freedomways
The Green Revolution
Guardian (New Left from 1967 on)
It Ain't Me, Babe
A Journal of Female Liberation
The Ladder: A Lesbian Review
Leviathan (formerly *Viet Report*)
Liberation
Liberator
LID News Bulletin

Lilith
Modern Utopian
Monthly Review
The Movement
New Left Notes
New Left Review
Off Our Backs
Our Generation
The Pedestal
Radical America
Ramparts
Rat
The Realist
Root and Branch
Socialist Register
Studies on the Left (1959–67)
Tangents (formerly *One Magazine*)
This Magazine Is About Schools
Up From Under
Vocations for Social Change
Win
Women: A Journal of Liberation

INDEX

185

This book has been set in 10 and 11 point Fairfield, leaded 2 and 3 points. Chapter numbers and titles are in 30 and 18 point Corvinus Medium #236. The size of the type page is 24 by 42½ picas.